River Stories

A collection of short fiction

Wayne Curtis

NIMBUS
PUBLISHING

Copyright © Wayne Curtis, 2000

All rights reserved. No part of this book may be reproduced, stored in a retrieval system or transmitted in any form or by any means without the prior written permission from the publisher, or, in the case of photocopying or other reprographic copying, permission from CANCOPY (Canadian Copyright Licensing Agency, 1 Yonge St, Suite 1900, Toronto, Ontario, M5E 1E5.

Nimbus Publishing Limited
PO Box 9301, Station A
Halifax, NS B3K 5N5
(902) 455-4286

Cover design: Heather Bryan/Margaret Issenman MGDC
Book design: Margaret Issenman MGDC
Photo Credits: Photos from the New Brunswick Public Archives and Mount Allison University Archives appear on pages 1, 2, 16, 24, 37, 38, 44, 57, 63, 73, 74, 78, 88, 101, 102, 112, and 122.
Printed and bound in Canada

Canadian Cataloguing in Publication Data
Curtis, Wayne, 1945–
River Stories
ISBN 1-555109-339-0

1. Miramichi River Region (N.B.) — Fiction. I. Title.
PS8555.U844T54 2000   C813'.54   C00-9500634
PR9199.3.C827T4 2000

Canadä
Nimbus Publishing acknowledges the financial support of the Canada Council and the Department of Canadian Heritage.

*For Carol Smith,
a coal lingering in the ash of old fantasies*

Acknowledgements

Some of the stories in this collection have appeared in the *New Brunswick Reader* and *The Atlantic Salmon Journal*. I would like to thank the New Brunswick Public Archives and Mount Allison University Archives for the use of photos. I would also like to thank the following people who offered me assistance in writing this book: Margaret Butler, Dennis Duffy, Fred Farrell, Joyce Hambrook, Larry Kennedy Sr., Jim Lorentz, and Carol Smith.

The characters in this book are products of the author's imagination. Any similarity to those living or dead is, as they say, purely coincidental.

Contents

Spring
Spring Days 2
When the Alder Leaf's a Mouse's Ear 16
Moving Shadows 24

Summer
The Raft 38
The Chambermaid's Daughter 44
Tight Lines 57
At the Superstore 63

Autumn
September Morning 74
A Fall Ailment 78
There Are Two Rivers Here 88

Winter
Lingering Melodies 102
At the Grand Hotel 112
Board Ice 122

Growth

In August
I walk
My father's fields
Amid wildflowers
Nodding
Ripe with seed.

His grey line fences
Gone
The wild chokecherry
Spreads magic
Over boundaries
From early years.

I squeeze
To where his plum trees
Used to grow
Now hidden.

I taste a small red plum
Recalling
When his trees were taller
The plums bigger
More tasty.

SPRING

Spring Days

Ice-out was what we had been waiting for since the first calendar day of spring. Every day after school, Harold Camp, Oxhana Hlodan and I walked to the river, across the fields behind my house, slumping along on shifting paths of coarse salt to stand and look at the ice, which had decayed ever so slightly from the day before. The first signs were along the shores. All winter this had been our skating ice, shovelled and tinted blue from the charcoal shade of trees. Now it was overflowed with urine-coloured water speckled with tree spills. The melting snow made the river rise and lift the ice to form a tapestry of craters with black-scrolled borders at underwater springs. Seeing a bit of open water, we had already asked our parents to write to Eaton's of Canada for new fishing hooks and lines.

"Remember the big salmon Oxhana caught on her way home from school last year," Harold said, grinning. "Hello for a circus." It was recess and we were outside without our coats, standing in the lee of the schoolhouse, out of the wind. Harold was pelting snowballs against the weathered boards of the woodshed where they stuck like frosted pies before melting in the sun to leave black velvet rivers.

"Yeah, she just let her line hang in the water as she walked across the wire bridge," I said, packing snow between my bare and aching hands.

"I took the big salmon home and Mom fried it for supper that night," Oxhana put in. "It was a bigger fish than any of us caught all spring, and I didn't even stop walking to hook it."

In the schoolyard we talked excitedly about what we had ordered from the catalogue, the black steel and split bamboo rods and the lines we would use on them. We reminisced about the juniper and black spruce poles we had fished with in past springs, and the old contraptions like rafts and kites we had used to get our lines out on the water. This took us away from the school work we loathed. We found ourselves reliving the experiences in whispers and giggles in the classroom, too, or contemplating where at the river we would go first when the ice had gone, until the disgusted teacher slammed a reader on her desk to get our attention.

After school we watched the advancing blackness along the shores and tossed sticks or snowballs onto the ice, which was growing paler with each sunny day. *A good rain is what we need,* my father had said. *A good sou'wester.* We prayed for this because the snow was melting so slowly.

Finally, the strips of open shore water became small rivers, and we could see them from our bedroom windows. Next we watched for the centre ice to crack then break away and set itself free. Harold, who had tired of waiting, fished in the open water along the shores. Sometimes he even caught a fish.

Meanwhile, we counted the days into April, compared the ice to that of other springs, and dreamed of the open river. At this time of year I did my evening chores with an ear and an eye to the river. I filled the kitchen woodbox, fed the hens, and helped my father in his store, all the while listening to freshet sounds, waiting for the vibration, the rumble of jamming ice.

One day during supper with my parents, the dishes in the buffet started to tinkle. I glanced at my father and without a word left the table, grabbed my coat and slumped through the rotting crust, stumbling and falling in boots filled with hail, to the shore where

Harold and Oxhana had already gathered to watch the ice going out. My heart was pounding.

We huddled, entranced by an angry avalanche of crowded angles cut with the precision of a protractor amid a river frothing wild from letting them go. The ice cracked as neatly as old-fashioned sugar frosting, then bumped, pushed, spilled, and up-ended in brown water to unfold our recurring dream. This dream of open water.

As if by some strange miracle, the puzzle separated and its pieces crowded the banks and pushed down trees, jamming ice houses, forts, and igloos into the woods at the high water mark. River wisdom said that if the jam left ice piled along the shores, the water would rise to these levels once more before the spring was over to clean it off. And whatever ice was left among the scarred and twisted trees above the high water mark would stay there, under the strengthening sun, to melt into heaps of coarse salt before dissolving into fertilizer and disappearing among the rocks and sand. Separated once more were our fox and geese circles, the skating rink, bonfire ashes, and exaggerated sled tracks made a little crazy by the sun so that they zigzagged and crossed to resemble the tracks of some lost or crazy giant.

The dirty water churned behind the jam while the heavy ice breaking made thumping sounds. The hollowness of the freshet echoed against the tracts of bare fields burnt black from hurried grass fires. The snow, soured from the day's warmth, already had a red-crusted sheen in the sunset. As a little breeze drifted in off the patches of open water, a duck flew up the river and a crow hollered behind us.

Yessir, we knew that this was real. This was spring, and not a winter's dream. There would be triangles, rectangles, and squares adrift for many days. But to us children the ice had gone from the river, from our minds. We stared at the open water, which the wind had coloured a metallic blue. We danced and hugged and were silly because our playground had been restored once again.

When we turned from the river we were lost in our own imaginings of boats and rafts, sails and kites, rods and fish. We tried in vain to sleep with these images dancing in our heads. It was as if some greater force had answered our prayers. Our place to swim, skip rocks, build sand castles, drift beneath stars, skinny dip, and fish had returned to us. Now we would watch it swell and cool after each rain, grow small and warm in dog days. But we would stay content within its green shores, seduced by sunsets of magic. We walked along the river's slopes first on last year's yellow hay, then on flats of sprouting green, and finally through reeds so tall we could not see each other, or ourselves. We knew that toward fall we would watch the grass fade to straw, the water to burnt crude oil. But for the moment, this was really the first day of spring.

After the tail end of the jam disappeared around the bend, even though the water was brown with debris, we hurried like crazy to prepare our fishing rods. We carefully picked our way over the windrows of ice along the shores to throw our first lines into the water. In places the ice would be two or three metres high with the sandy water lapping against it. In other places there would be a greasy metre of bare shore in front of the ice, where the backwater had already dropped away. And there would be ice slabs jutting out into the water, slabs we would stand on to cast our lines well out into the heavy flow. It seemed there was always a cold wind coming off the water on the first days after ice-out, turning the water to ink and making little white-crested waves in contrast to the ice still adrift.

This wind made it hard for us to get a line out when we were trying to reach as far as we could to hook that first spring salmon. Our parents warned us not to stand on the ice or in front of the miniature icebergs that sometimes crumbled from the heat of the sun and slid into the water. They knew that if we were in front of one of these and it started to slide, we could be swept into the river, maybe even driven to the bottom and pinned there under its tonnage. Although the idea of being in that muddy water as cold as ice was terrifying, it did not deter us from our fishing.

Harold, who lived just across the river from me, had been swept into Charlie's Eddy by ice that avalanched, and he lived to tell about it. He had been standing on a slab, casting to where he had seen a fish raise, when the whole concern started to slide, pushing him a good three metres from the shore into the murky water. His only injury was a sprained ankle, and he was able to swim in close enough so I could help pull him out. He limped home to get dry clothes and was back at the river in less than an hour.

For the month or so following ice-out, Harold, Oxhana—who also lived across the river by way of the wire bridge—and I would fish spring salmon on Saturdays and Sundays and until dark every evening after school. Sometimes I would catch a salmon from the wire bridge on my way to meet them at Charlie's Eddy just below home. As I walked the footbridge high above the water, I would strip line off the reel and let it down over the side then move along briskly to let the big streamer—a Smelt or a Golden Eagle—troll across the water a hundred metres downstream. Trolling wasn't legal on our river yet; of course, fishing from a bridge was always illegal. So I never stopped on the bridge but kept walking with my line in the water. I could see my fly trailing along behind my yellow casting line and the leader.

When the fly swung over a certain place, depending on the water's height and how early or late in the spring it was, a swell might come after it, then I would feel the fish's pull. I would pull back hard and concentrate on keeping my tip up while running towards the far abutment, down the steps onto the grassy shore to pick up some of the line and eventually land the fish. Ninety-nine percent of these salmon I released, even back then. My parents would not eat them, and I was warned not to bring them home.

We would come in from the river at dark, our faces chapped from the wind, our hands red from the cold, and with energetic voices tell our parents about the evening's fish. There was always excitement in our voices when we talked about the river.

"Harold and I both hooked the same fish," I told my father in the store one night.

"You what?" he asked, not looking up from his work.

"Yeah, we hooked the same fish at the same time, Harold and I. Our lines must have been crossed and the flies hooked together before the salmon struck. We had a lot of line out when it happened. It was funny because I was arguing with Harold that my fish was bigger than his. But then we noticed that everywhere his fish went, mine followed. That's how we knew it was the same fish."

"I've had that happen," Father said while he continued to work. "So who claimed the fish?"

"Harold. I gave it to him because he seemed to feel the pull a few seconds before I did. It didn't really matter because we let it go anyway."

"That's the boy."

Later in the spring we would fish more deliberately under the wire bridge and share a pack of Matinee or Export cigarettes I had stolen from my father's store. Sometimes Harold and I would hide in the bushes under the bridge to look up the skirts of the girls who walked across on their way home from school. On windy days they would have to hold their skirts with one hand and hold on to the cabled railing with the other. Once the girls told the teacher what we were doing, and for the week that followed she kept us in twenty minutes longer than the girls each afternoon. The teacher warned us to keep away from the bridge after school—the worst possible punishment for us at that time of the spring, when fishing was good and time was lost sitting in school.

Our footbridge was like a large wire hammock that stretched across the river between a crib work of field stone and cedar on each riverbank, with plank steps coming down from each end. Its four steel cables were netted in with page wire, and at the centre the boards were wired to crosspieces of two-by-fours. In summer the bridge swung a good ten metres above the water and we would jump from it into the salmon hole below. But during the spring freshet, the bridge was often sitting on the water. I can remember hearing it from my bedroom, slapping and swishing on the angry night river, and I would pray for its survival. Sometimes the bridge was caught in ice floes or other debris and ripped from its abutments to hang along one shore with its boards bleaching in the sun like a defeated giant's backbone. We would walk the banks on different sides of the river, waiting for the government men to come and put our world back together. Later, a pier was built in the centre of the river and the bridge became two short, higher hammocks.

Although the bridge became a favourite hang-out, we had miles of river to play on. Except for a few American fishermen from some river camp with a guide who always anchored well out from shore, the river was mostly left to us children before fly-fishing for spring salmon had caught on with the locals. Otherwise, only a few adults ventured to the river to take a look at the water and then go back to work in their yards. They were waiting for the gaspereau and shad and the giant runs of sea trout that came with them. And the bright salmon.

We seldom used a boat to fish. We didn't own a decent one. Harold was always tinkering with an old boat of his father's, which we would struggle to put into the river every once in a while, but it always leaked in spite of what we did. Oxhana and I helped him hammer in the oakum, boil tar, and paint over the cracks with a chip. Still, it was not safe even to go out two or three metres from shore. Sometimes we would put the boat's bow up on the shore, the stern in the water, and take turns standing on it to fish. This put us out a bit farther.

Eventually, we used the old boat as a windbreak, propping it on its gunwale among the shore alders. We sat on the upriver side on the warm grass to keep an eye on the river, watching for a salmon to jump or roll. Harold, Oxhana, and I would smoke at the river while we fished. Harold would tell some dirty story or sing an old whorehouse song. I thought they were funny, but Oxhana always blushed. If the wind was blowing the right way, we would fix our streamers and lines to the frame of a kite, get it into the air, and let the wind take it out over the middle of the river, then jerk the hook free and reel in slowly. We caught many salmon kite-fishing on windy spring days.

When it was calm, Harold Camp would lay out his long cast in slow motion, straight as an arrow with the fly lighting softly twenty or more metres out. We had to learn to cast long and straight because we were on a big river and without a boat. There is no greater motivation to learn to cast than a big fish rolling and jumping on the surface just beyond reach. I enjoyed watching Harold. Even now, I would just as soon sit and watch a good caster as do it myself. I suppose it goes back to when we very young and had to share one rod among us.

We pretty much gave up on the idea of getting out on the water. We had cut the shore bushes with an axe to make room to cast, and we stood on boulders at the top of eddies and runs to cast into the flow as far out as we could. I can remember sitting on a fence abutment on the bank, watching Harold stand at the edge of the water at Charlie's and hook twelve grilse one sunny April evening. It was a great advantage to be up high when we were watching for fish to move; I saw some of those fish coming for the fly long before he did.

I distinctly remember a certain fly rod Harold and I shared, a department store split-bamboo with a yellow casting line, a too-short leader, and a few streamers we bummed from the old guides who hung out at my father's store. The guides always had streamers in the bands of their hats in the spring. There was an intimacy between us kids and these men because we were sharing the river. A nod or a wink triggered an experience we had shared. Most of the fly hooks they passed on to us—Smelts, Mickey Finns, and Golden Eagles—would have been given to the guides for safe-keeping by some sportsman who had already gone back to the States, perhaps never to return. When my father wasn't looking, we smoked their tobacco. Because of this solidarity we made a point to hang out at the store and talk with them about fishing, and which streamers were the most effective. The guides dressed in wool pants and high river boots and wore broad felt hats. We all wanted to be guides when we grew up.

If we couldn't get fly hooks at the store, we would attempt to tie our own, using black steel bait hooks and wrapping on the feathers of hens and ducks from my father's barn. If we were able to get to the village, which was just six kilometres from home, we could buy a Dell comic book and a trout fly for a quarter at Bean and Dumphy's general store. An Oriole, a Dusty Miller, a Kid Colt, a Wyatt Earp. Since we shared a fishing rod, whomever was not fishing sat in the lee of the overturned boat to read the comic books and smoke. Oxhana and I traded comic books because Harold wasn't a reader, and we exchanged fly hooks among ourselves the way children might trade hockey or baseball cards today. Each of us had our own little collection. We compared the success of the fly hooks, tale against tale, while we savoured the flavour of stolen cigarettes. I still associate fly hooks, comic books, and cigarettes with the river whenever I see them in a store. If I am in a smoke shop, I find myself looking for a certain brand, even though I have not used tobacco for years. The flies, books, and tobacco come together and take me to that old river again.

Lou Butterfield, an American whose lodge was about a kilometre or so above my home, was an expert fly-tier. He had built himself a small tackle shop on the riverbank near his lodge. The building was full of fly-tying materials, paddles, poles, and scoop nets. One year his shop went adrift in the spring run-off. It drifted, sitting upright like some kind of crazy houseboat. The currents brought it to shore on the flat in back of Charlie's Eddy where it caught in the bushes. When the water fell and we discovered what it was, Harold, Oxhana and I brought pry bars and poles to straighten it into place. We were careful to leave it hidden in the trees. We used it all that summer as our own private tackle shop. It eliminated the fly hook problem, at least for the time. I can still see Harold coming through the doorway of that shop with an ungodly fly hook he had tied from the wealth of exotic feathers and yarns there. Mr. Butterfield looked for his shop in vain, inquiring of people along the river. Of course, no one had seen it. The following spring the high water took the shack from us and deposited it on some other property further downriver.

One Saturday morning in April, when we had tarred Harold's father's old boat for the hundredth time and put it in the river, it did not seem to be leaking much. We had never heard of life jackets, so Harold and I took only our rods and pushed the boat out in the river about three metres, where the Americans fished and dropped anchor. Our anchor was a ten-pound oblong rock that was tethered to a ten-metre chain. We sat fishing and smoking, letting the sun beam down on us like we had seen the Americans do, while we talked in Yankee accents. We let our line out and reeled it through the eddy, keeping our gaze in the vicinity of the fly hooks, waiting for the big pull.

There was a sudden gentle nudge from behind us. My first thought was that this was one of Harold's tricks, even though he was in front of me looking downriver. We turned quickly to see a slab of ice the size of a hockey rink crosswise against our boat, pushing us at the speed of the water. We knew that the proper thing to do in this emergency, according to our guide friends, was cut the anchor rope, quickly. But we were using a chain, and there was no pulley to lift the anchor. So we drifted, ice and boat, the anchor dragging on the bottom. We were hoping the ice would swing off, and we pushed against it with the paddle.

Then what we feared most happened. The anchor caught on the bottom and held fast, and the ice splintered into the soggy old boat, yanking half the bow under it. Harold and I clung desperately to what was left of the boat, cradling it against the ice as we tried to push ice and boat scraps to shore. I was very frightened by then, and I relied on Harold's judgement because he was older and seemed to know more about the river than I did. Or so I thought.

I would have jumped and tried to swim had he not said, "Don't move! Sit tight!"

I shiver even now when I think of this little secret we kept from our parents for all these years, and I wake in the night in a cold sweat. But at the time we kept calm and sat tight and hung with the boat as, inch by inch, the whole concern started to move closer to shore, where we could make the jump, getting only our feet wet. We were only a kilometre downriver, just above Dead Man's Hole, where it was said people had drowned because there was an undertow and no bottom. Since then, I never get into a boat without first checking its anchor rope and pulley.

On an evening in May, Harold stood fishing on the end of another old boat. He had borrowed his brother Lloyd's black steel rod. When the boat tipped, Howard fell overboard, and he stayed under for a long time while I danced up and down in a panic. Finally his blond head emerged three or four metres downstream. As I shouted he swam like a beaver toward me and crawled shivering up on the grassy shore. He stood dripping and belching, wiping the water out of his eyes. Then he sat on the grass to wring the water out of his wool socks. He looked like a wild man. Then he barked his one-syllable *Ha!* and I knew he was all right.

I realized then that something was missing. I said to him, "Harold, you lost the rod!"

"Oh God," he said, "that rod belongs to Lloyd. He doesn't know I borrowed it. If I go home without it, I'll be shot!" Without hesitation he jumped in again, went under for what seemed like minutes before he finally came up with the rod's cork in his teeth. He was pale as a corpse as he put on his wet coat and stomped toward home, the rod dragging behind.

Later that same spring an uncle of Harold's gave him a small canvas canoe in exchange for a cord of firewood cut into stove lengths and split, and a promise to keep his garden weeded through the summer. This little boat was very tipsy and would not safely accommodate more than one person. Oxhana refused to get in it, but Harold and I fished out of it. We would sit square in the middle on the bottom and had to work constantly to keep it balanced while we paddled, especially if there was a wind.

One afternoon, we set out in it for Vickers Pool, which was two kilometres below our community. As we paddled against the wind, out around the middle pier, towards the declining sun, the upriver breeze moved the water in patches of black, and the sun scattered broken crystals. We fished the evening but saw nothing. To bring the boat upstream, we fashioned a sail by tying our shirts together between two horizontal poles and let the wind push us. As we drifted along with the wind at our backs, Howard sang a rowdy song from *Down at the Red Light Saloon.*

Along with raunchy lyrics, Harold always enjoyed a good practical joke. Later in the spring an American gave Harold a pair of pant-waders for helping him land a salmon at Charlie's Eddy. He came to the river with the waders under his pants. The river was a long way above summer-low and cold—there was still snow in the woods.

"That water's not cold tonight," Harold called after he was in for awhile. "C'mon, wade in." I waded out to my waist to stand beside him.

After a few minutes I said, "Look, this is too cold for me. I can't stand it!" Harold started to laugh. Later he lifted his jeans to show me the rubber wading boots underneath.

Sometimes on Saturday afternoons, after washing up in the river using cupped hands and drying our faces on our sleeves, we would go up the hill to Harold's mother's house for a lunch. In their small unpainted summer kitchen, with its sagging porch a rank smell of smoke and fried fish, we ate off a ketchup-and-molasses-stained tablecloth. It seemed there was always a fry pan filled with salmon steaks on the cook stove, and an aluminum pot filled with boiled potatoes that had the peelings left on. Harold's mother was generally busy somewhere, so we would help ourselves. Harold's old dog, Rowdy, smelling the way that old dogs do, would groan and pant and crowd around us while we ate.

By the time I had reached my teens, I had become bored with life on the river. I can remember meeting Harold at the river on May mornings, and even though the conditions were right and we were hooking a few fish, I wanted to leave. I paced the shore, restless, but I stayed awhile longer because I did not want to insult Harold, who was standing by the boat casting the same way he had done since I started fishing with him years before. But something was wrong. I could not put my finger on. Maybe I had grown away from the river. Maybe I was missing Oxhana, who had gone away a year or so ahead of me. I made a few more casts before I walked down the shore.

"What, leavin' sa soon?" Harold called after me. "The fishin's good. Stand here where I am and try it."

"No, no. Just going for a little walk Harold. I'll be back."

"I have tobacco. Here, make yourself a cigarette." He held out his tobacco.

"That's okay. I have some."

It seems that spring I had grown away from the boyhood pleasures I had lived for. I wanted to leave the country, go to the city, something everyone of my generation was doing then. Everyone except Harold, who stayed at the river.

When I returned from Ontario a few years later the wire bridge had been washed away by spring floods which were flowing out of different woods, indeed, over a different landscape. The river had become inhabited by a different kind of people. Many of them had come from the city to get away from the responsibility and stress of earning a living. But Harold was still there fishing among them and griping about the intrusions they had brought.

Harold died from leukemia in the Moncton Hospital at the age of fifty-five. I went to see him there. He laid in the bed twisted and thin, and I sat beside him. We reminisced about the old days and the river. He filled me in on the years I had missed, the years he wished I had been there with him to experience more of the same.

Now when I go to the river, I can feel Harold Camp there beside me, his freckled face beaming as he pulls a large trout or salmon out of the eddy. I can still smell his tobacco smoke. He is swearing, laughing, singing those rowdy old songs. Sometimes Oxhana Hlodan is there with us, and we are fixing a sail to an old boat. Or we are listening to Harold sing as we prepare to string a line off the wire bridge. These memories of Harold and Oxhana have withstood the passing of time. But ageing, like winter, comes hard in the country. It happens fast. Oh, fast. And it seems that in the country there is never anything along the way to take the place of childhood.

"Oh, they were great years," he said. "Ya shoulda stayed around, Jimmy." He took a cigarette and offered me one. We leaned together to light them with one match like we used to do. When I got up to leave, he said, "What, leavin' us sa soon?" So I sat down for a few minutes more.

When the Alder Leaf's a Mouse's Ear

I have always associated spring fishing with potato planting. By late spring, towards June, there were patches of green grass and dandelions in the lee of buildings where the sun was strongest. Even this far into the season, the wind was cool. We had to wear our jackets when we went to the river. At this time of year Harold Camp, Oxhana Hlodan and I would give a written excuse to our teacher for a couple of days off from school to help our parents with the planting. Two days off could grow into three or four simply by encouraging our parents to let us help them with other seasonal jobs. There were many around home. I still relate sunny spring weather to those days, out of school, planting vegetables and grain—and the river. I have tied them together.

    We gathered angle worms from behind my father's plough as he stumbled along behind the horse, turning up the orange clay so we could sprinkle fists of fertilizer before dragging a chain to mix it into grey ash and drop in the potato seed, each one with its eyes turned upward, and with just one sandal track between them. Planting was tiring work. Oxhana, Harold and I helped each other on our respective farms to shorten our work day. Of course, the potato seed would have been cut by my grandfather. For only he knew this delicate and important art. He would sit upon a wheelbarrow at the edge of the field, carefully looking over each potato before cutting into it at different angles, making sure there was at least one eye in a seed. The brand of these potatoes, after so many generations, he did not know well himself. Nobody knew. But they were sweet tasting and without rot, and we planted them in quantities large enough to last our family the winter. Whatever happened to us in the way of hard times, we would always have plenty of potatoes and fish—gaspereau, shad, salmon.

When the planting was done, or nearly done, we would wander off one at a time, stealing over the hill when my father's back was turned and then run to the river. We always went separately, trying to seem inconspicuous. We would whisper a message as we passed in a drill, *You take the worms and I'll meet you there as soon as I can get away.* Some of the strongest images I have from my boyhood are of Oxhana and Harold running like the breeze to the river, all of us huddling together to light cigarettes, and our fathers trudging innocently behind their horses, planting, cultivating, harvesting. I can still feel the grit of clay and fertilizer under my nails, the wiggle of sand-coated angel worms crowded into my shirt pocket, bait when the day's work was done. I can still taste the cigarettes and the fish scales, as well as the medicated ointments my mother used to apply to our hands and lips, which had become chapped from water and wind.

Perhaps the escape from school, the freedom, brought garden and river together in this way. Certainly, we depended on both and they were equally important. But we loved the river most because it had become *the* place to get away, free from our work at home that we had used as an excuse to break free from school.

This little respite would come shortly after Arbor Day, when the schoolyard had been raked and we were bored with reviewing decimals and fractions and studying literature and history for our final exams. We had been counting the days until school was let out in the third week of June. I can still recall the school songs our teacher used to fill in the time: "Juanita," "Way Down Upon the Swanee River," "My Old Kentucky Home Far Away."

By that time the bright salmon would be in the river. Everybody knew that once the gaspereau came in, the sea trout came with them, and the Rocky Brook salmon were not far behind. We never saw the Rocky Brook fish. We only heard about them from parents and neighbours. Someone fishing for spring trout would have hooked one or maybe had the good fortune of finding one tangled in a gaspereau net. We never knew the Rocky Brook fish to jump or show itself on our part of the river. So they remained a legend, the ideal fish, considered the fattest and best tasting of them all.

In the spring, we would bait fish in the eddies. Our lines and hooks and floats were bought at the five-and-dime store in town, our juniper rods cut and dragged from the swamp on the crust of March, and stood against the woodshed to dry in the sun. We had watched my grandfather dry pickets as well as the cedar posts he had sawn into short blocks and hewn into hexagons and octagons, then drilled to make floats for the gaspereau net. My grandfather, at age eighty-seven, had his own projects. I learned a lot from him about practical things.

Sometimes I would have a day off from school to help with the important job of preparing nets for the spring catch. I remember standing proudly beside my grandfather, untangling the fine twine and holding the two-inch mesh up to his failing eyes as he simmed it to the long tarred rope we had strung along the clothesline. He used a big wooden needle wrapped in figure eights of twine. We built a fire on the ground to burn the sharp edges off the floats and blacken them. We knew the gaspereau were running because the alder leaf had grown to the size of a mouse's ear. That also meant it was time to whittle fish needles from a cedar shingle and make a picket maul from a block of maple.

Tarring Grandfather's boat was another springtime ritual I enjoyed. Oakum ropes, tapping hammers, and drums of boiling tar; I can still smell the twine, ropes, dyes, tar, oakum, and paint for the old board boat. There was the right way to tar a boat and no other way. To make sure the standards were kept, the crucial chores were left mostly to the experienced elderly. But with a bright young lad along to observe. . . .

The pickets were driven off our shore and the gaspereau net was strung out at the same time every spring. When the water dropped they would drive more pickets to put the net further out. The old-timers of our community would come around to sit with my grandfather under a lean-to at the shore, and they would whittle and smoke, chew their tobacco and sip brandy to drive off the chill for the week or so the fishery lasted, or until everyone got their fill of the scaly, bony fish. They would sit and watch the water bubble around the pickets, waiting for the floats to bob under, a sure sign the net was heavy with fish. Then each man, with a chew of tobacco in cheek, would get into the boat. One would grind the pole into the rocky bottom, the others would overhaul the net, taking out the fish and remarking that some of them were already getting soft and thin while the water in the river was still good and cold. *And if you don't think that water's cold mister man, just jump in there and see how long you can stand it.* Even though the water in the river was truly warming by then and the gaspereau were soft in the bellies, the old men would laugh and come ashore with the boat's bottom alive and kicking.

These fish were scaled and gutted in the brook nearby. Their bellies were filled with salt, and the fish were placed in circles, layer upon layer, until the small wooden barrels were full. Fish to be smoked or cooked a dozen different ways through the winter, served with potatoes cooked a dozen different ways. A crony of my grandfather's, George Jardine, used to joke that he could get a mess of gaspereau on his side of the river by standing on the shore with a leaf rake and hauling them in. *Ha, haaaa. That's a good one George!*

On the shore above home, halfway between the potato field and the eddy, there was an old cedar log raft, complete with benches, that had been there for years. It was jammed between two shore willows at the high water level, on the slope of dusty dead grass and sprouting ferns. Harold, Oxhana, and I would sit on the raft and pretend we were drifting, our eyes half-closed so that we could glance sideways at the choppy river. Sometimes a motorboat would breeze by and corrugate the surface. We rafted across an ocean of freedom many times on that log raft, riding the waves that came with each passing boat.

Ours was a big river, with big trees and big fish. The Cavanaugh Eddy was very deep, even in close. Patches of foam drifted upstream in tiny whirlpools and twisted outward to catch in the main flow, hold momentarily and drift away. The sand and rocky shore seemed to stay warm from the sun even on the cool breezy days. A large pine tree stooped over the water there. Its outstretched limbs kept us dry on wet days, and shaded on sunny days. Its roots, like exposed arms and legs, kinked and twisted in all directions, growing into the riverbank. In spots these roots were scarred and splintered from the ice runs. Beneath the gnarled tangle was a place to crawl into. The woodchucks that we spooked from that place whistled and scolded and scampered in a frenzy. We could look up through a whispering reach of pine needles to the sky, where silver bullets made chalk vapour trails that drifted slowly across an opaque blue field. From the outside, we could hook our feet under one of the roots to let our heads hang down, making the river look like a tilted and moving ceiling of crystals. When the water warmed, we would swing from a rope tied to one of those limbs, swishing well out and splashing down into the eddy to swim back to shore.

Here we used our juniper rods to cast pastel lines, their steel hooks smothered in angle worms, toward the outer flow. The lines twisted upstream and downstream then up again before curling slowly to the bottom. We stuck our rods into the sandy shore and took our places in the shadows of the great tree with bunion roots while we smoked and watched for a jerk of the line. On a bright day, we would climb high into the pine limbs where we could see fish far below through the amber water, milling about on the bottom, their tails moving like flags blowing in a wind. The flash of a fish's side could give away the presence of a spring salmon in the eddy, a tell-tale sign of why smaller fish were not biting.

When the eddy was stacked with shad like a department store aquarium, we sometimes jigged one for excitement. These looked like gaspereau but were much larger. We dreamed of the day when we would be able to afford decent fly rods so we could cast over this same water and hook a Rocky Brook salmon, maybe even a large speckled trout. On those April and May evenings, always just before dark, the trout came in and took our baited hooks.

In my mother's and grandmother's wallpapered kitchen, I would negotiate for just one more day of my spring break from school because the vegetable garden needed to be planted. Of course, the truer motivation was that I had become intoxicated by the river and hanging out there with the older kids. I pointed out that the seeds had to go into the ground immediately because there was rain in the forecast and once it started, it could last for a week or more. Besides, a long spring rain gave the seeds the start they needed. I sensed even then that parents took great pride in knowing their garden seeds were sprouting ahead of some others in the community.

As promised, the next day my friends and I helped drop tiny purple seeds into the ground and dust the clay over them with the heel of a garden rake. Little envelopes with pictures of beets and carrots and turnips were displayed on stakes at drill's end. Then, one by one, Harold, Oxhana and I disappeared, stealing away to the river.

From the Cavanaugh Eddy we could hear my father shouting as he half stumbled, half staggered behind the horse, working on into the twilight, harrowing the flats close by for oat planting. In the early morning, before the wind came up and if the rain held off, I knew he would sow the oats. Pace and sow, pace and sow, stiff-legged, with arms swinging like a Russian soldier, casting the grain over the corduroy earth. Next he would harrow in the seeds, changing the sand from powdered chocolate to mahogany. The rain-dimpled clay would fade to powder once more as the grain started to sprout. Beat the weather. It seems my father was always trying to beat the weather. With planting grain, there was nothing really that we children could do to help him.

So, with the red sky setting farmhouse windows ablaze and the darkness of the post-sunset crowding in upon us, we sat in the pine roots by a river of moving tar and listened to peepers in the swamp, the warble of a nesting robin or a faraway bird that the old people called a "clinker." *A great bird the clinker, the voice of spring,* my father would say. We could never see it and even now it remains more a sound than a bird. But we could scent the newly turned earth on the same breeze that carried the shouting, shouting. Beat the weather. My father loved his land and what it would yield for him. And he loved his horse. We knew that when we came up from the river at dark, he would be in the barn, perhaps with a lantern, going over the horse's rump with a curry comb. He would stop what he was doing to admire our catch, however small, comment on what a great river it was, how lucky we were to have it running by our door. My father and grandfather could tell by the smell of the river if the water was rising or falling. They could tell by the echoes if it were going to rain.

My grandfather and his cronies, after almost a week, would still be sitting by the river, fishing the net because a neighbour's barrel was not yet full. Even though the water had warmed and the gaspereau were as soft as fiddler's farts, these men were also trying to beat the weather. A hollowness in the air, the voices of certain birds, and wild animals feeding along the shores all meant rain. A storm would bring the water up and the gaspereau would be running crazy to hell and all over the river. The pickets would have to come down because the muddy water would fill the net with grass and sand and sticks. Everything would have to be stored in a shed—nets and pickets, benches and barrels—because the fishery would be over for another year, if not forever.

In the meantime, the old men hunched on a bench in the dusk and sipped brandy, their pipes of sweet tobacco glowing. Their warm sweaters, buttoned up to the throat, made them look like old roosting birds. They joked and savoured the evening while the floats bobbed or stayed under for maybe the last time. Then they would get up from the bench and go out to look at the net once more.

Their voices would carry on the water up to the eddy, where Harold, Oxhana and I, cradled in the arms of the pine tree, watched our lines. We listened to their poles bump against the boat, the slap of fish, the old men's raspy voices.

"Hold your jaw Jake, there's a good one Davie!"

"Here's lookin' at ya George!" They were sipping still from the jug of brandy.

"And I'll never see my Nellie anymore," Grandfather sang.

And I think, for the very young and the very old, a river is the place to be.

Moving Shadows

You see, often I live in those days of endless sunshine, wind, and river that Oxhana, Harold and I possessed long before our school days had begun. Old coins or arrowheads carried in a handkerchief, brought out and examined once in a while—shadows I call them. They are unbidden, even unconscious. I hang on to things, even now, like nobody else I know. I can almost taste that old-world river, the shore grass, and the smell of fish and hot gravel. Even the scent of the new-turned clay from my father's harrowed fields and the smoke of stolen cigarettes live in these shadows, projected by what has become an articulate slanting sun.

I think of those shadows now as I work in my yard, going over the grounds with a garden rake, collecting the pine buds and the spills that have accumulated from the past winter. It's a nice change in pace after a long hard day in a furniture store. The evening sun is hot and I take off my jacket and throw it to land in a heap on the veranda steps. Then I sit and light a cigarette.

Across the river I can hear voices at the mouth of Hlodan's Brook, Oxhana, her three sisters and two brothers, and my own young self among them, standing at the edge of the water, bantering over position the way we used to as children fishing trout. Behind the Hlodan's unpainted wooden house, I can see Oxhana's father Harry in his flannel shirt and felt hat going back and forth across the field behind his team of horses, tired and heavy from the long day's ploughing. My father (less visible right now) is preparing his fields on this side, where he will be planting potatoes and grain to compare and contrast with Harry's. Everything is more vivid now because the Hlodan family have gathered this evening in their yard at the old home for a potluck supper to honour Oxhana's funeral. She was buried in the south of India after she died there of an aneurysm at age fifty-two.

I must go inside to write a sympathy card to Mrs Hlodan, I think. Like Oxhana's family, I was not able to get to her funeral. For this reason I am unable to put her to rest. It seems her life has always been a part of my own, even though I have not seen her much since school days.

Oxhana and I were born three days apart in early February 1943. Because the river separated our farms it became a symbol that I knew would always be a big part of us both. I still have a clear image of Oxhana as a kid, freckled and tanned in ragged shorts and bare feet. She would whistle from her shore by holding a blade of grass between her palms and blow through them when she wanted me to come play.

At the river we would build castles in the mud, trap baby eels, and gather empty clam shells to skip on the water. When we played hide and seek in the woods, Oxhana would squat long enough to pee in the pine needles then keep running. Once, she led me to the meadow and showed me her big secret: a robin's nest. It was well hidden among powdery apple tree leaves. As we stretched to see the eggs, the mother robin scolded and chased us away. Afterwards we stood against the same old tree and put our arms around each other, playing "house." When I recall that moment now, I believe the hug may have come later; time compresses a thing after a while. It must have been later still that we lay in the grass, where it seems the breeze was always soothing like a piece of music, and planned our future together, living in a mansion somewhere in a storybook land. Sometimes we played King and Queen. I would give her a bouquet of blue violets and kneel on scabby knees before her as she took the flowers in her dirty hands.

These shadows appear and disappear in tiny flashes when I'm at the river now. Images and symbols set them spinning so that Oxhana and I are etched in a riverscape that flows deep inside me from out of the past. I can see us jumping naked from rafts, slipping and sliding underwater like silk against granite. At the river I gave her my first poems, rolled up in bullet shells to keep them dry. This is where we sang our favourite song that went, "Beautiful, beautiful brown eyes…"—we both had brown eyes. Even now when I come here I can hear our singing in the hum of the wires and the wind, in the sigh of trees. Our laughter is in the chuckle of water. Oxhana and I had shared the same pew in church, the same class in school. We had followed the same miniature rainbows in a sense. Now the shadows repeat it all like we have been cast in an intriguing old film, freeze-framed in the black and white of long ago.

There was a time when we were in school that I didn't like Oxhana very much. In grade four, I thought she had become a tattle-tale and was full of the devil. She was the one who told our teacher that Harold and I were hiding under the bridge to watch the girls walk over on their way home from school. For this the teacher had kept us after class. But by the time we were twelve, Oxhana and I had became friends again, this time in a slightly different way.

Oxhana's mother, our teacher, was a mother to us all. But at school Mrs. Hlodan was mundane and dry and, to me, always incomprehensible, in spite of her efforts. But she was careful never to favour her own children so that everyone felt equal in the schoolhouse. Oxhana and I sat across from each other. I realize now that I orchestrated this because she would share her answers with me, holding her notes at an angle so that I could read, especially if she knew I had not studied and was having trouble. Back then I missed a lot of school because of asthma. She seemed to be more intelligent, too, the way that girls always used to be, or she tried harder. Her knowledge gave her a kind of power over me. I had the impression then that I was a heart not a mind person, and because I was small and suffered from asthma, especially in the spring of the year when the snow was melting, I felt that Oxhana could have been physically stronger than me, too. Yet she was never condescending and because of this, by the time I had reached my early teens I had plucked many petals from daisies to end in her favour. *She loves me. She loves me not. She loves me.*

My mother never fully approved of me playing with Oxhana because she swore like a trooper, a sign of further unladylike things she would do. But in our small community, playmates were not to be rejected easily. We became defiant, even inseparable. Our friendship was sealed on a Thursday afternoon in February of grade six, when Oxhana kept me from getting the strap. During a Junior Red Cross meeting, we had been throwing paper missiles that carried notes to one another. One of my missiles accidentally glided toward the teacher's desk. Mrs. Hlodan picked it up and glanced at it. *I think that you have the cutest bum in the school.* She gasped and I watched closely as her face flushed. When she finally spoke, her B-flat voice hit pitches of E-sharp and beyond.

"I'm so shocked!" she cried. "I know the boy who wrote this. He comes from a respectable family. I'm so disappointed in him. I'm asking that student to stay in school when the class is dismissed."

I knew that Mrs. Hlodan had recognized my writing, but I tried not to show it. As everyone filed out of the schoolhouse at the end of the meeting, she caught my arm.

"I think the one who wrote the note knows to whom I am speaking."

Oxhana, who was beside me, stopped and told her mother that the note had been directed at her, that she had written similar notes to me, and that if I had to stay in, she would stay also and be punished. We got a lecture but were spared the strap.

The next morning, in an adolescent kind of contempt, we jigged school to skate on the river because it was Valentine's Day. Spring was not far off and we knew the good ice wouldn't last, and this was after a cold night that had followed a big rain. I thought then that I loved Oxhana Hlodan. After the school incident, there seemed to be a double victory in our plan.

To get out of school, Oxhana had pretended to be sick. I had left home with my books and taken a shortcut through the swamp, across the frozen river. After nine o'clock, when Mrs. Hlodan and the others were in school, I went to Oxhana's house. There in the warmth of her low-ceiling wainscot kitchen, which was made even more inviting by the wrath of frost outside, between a derelict water pump and the cluttered wood range, I got my first kiss. Ever. It was secret and magic and it made my insides tingle. But it was quickly followed by a wave of guilt as though I had done something terribly wrong. I wondered briefly if I should let it happen again. Within minutes I was following Oxhana for more of the same. She went into her mother's bedroom, which was embroidered with doilies and smelled of perfumes and face powders. I stood watching as she dabbed on her mother's lipstick then sprayed cologne on the front of her sweater, cologne that smelled like my mother's Lily of the Valley. We put on our skates in the kitchen and walked to the pond, leaving our slashes in the crust. The river was wide at our favourite place, slow moving in summer, and Oxhana always referred to it as "the pond."

On the river ice it was cold but sunny and bright with a sprinkling of crystals that sparkled when we faced into the sun. We skated on frosted glass and the ringing of our skates cut through the morning air like arrows. As we skated around the black shores in places of underwater springs, I thought of the summer river beneath us and the fish we had tried to capture, now in their comatose winter state. There was the ever-present smell of chimney smoke and sometimes even cow manure, sharp and sour, in an aimless wind. And the smell of Oxhana's cologne.

We skated, first apart then arm in arm, keeping time in an easy morning stride to an inner music. The winter sun cast our moving shadows before us, shadows that for me have brought Oxhana and I together a thousand times since, lengthening, twisting and darkening as the time passed, first blue, then charcoal, then black. It seemed that Oxhana could anticipate my next move, even before I could, as if for her it was all an exercise in habit. She could dictate the pace, even here.

We played tag. Oxhana would skate up behind me, lock her arms around my waist and squeeze so I could feel her warmth beneath the layers of clothing, smell her perfume. When I turned to kiss her again, she pulled away. So we skated, and I worked to make my weight shift with hers. Then she stopped. This time we kissed. Though her lips were cold, they were soft and full, and warming to me.

When our feet started to ache from the cold we built a bonfire near the trees at the foot of Taylors Mountain. Seated on our mittens on the ice, we took off our skates and held our wool socks to the blaze, rubbing and massaging out the short painful spasms of pins and needles to bring the feeling back into our feet. I had a pack of stolen Matinees from my father's store. As we smoked, the river, the woods, and indeed our families disappeared. I realize only now, so many years later, just how great an influence Oxhana really was. At the time I did not even notice her dimpled innocent smile, her moving brown eyes, her black hair held in a ponytail by a rubber band. I did not see her for who she was, the way she was so close to home.

Oxhana would never completely agree with anything I said, even if I had the facts, but she would come up with a philosophy of her own that was close to mine. She was more forward and open than I, but had a strong sense of responsibility from being raised poor, more so than I ever did, even though my family was poor too. Because her father, Harry, was a diabetic and had lost some of his eyesight by then, it seemed Oxhana could find no reprieve from the chores on the Hlodan farm. I had seen her milk a cow before going to school, carry in the day's firewood, or on a Saturday afternoon take the axe to the barn to kill a hen for the Sunday meal, a task that I had been spared. But she always seemed preoccupied with a bigger concern, a dream of the future she was nurturing.

"I want to be a singer when I grow up," she said as we sat warming our feet. "No, I think maybe I want to be an actor or a producer. That's it, a movie producer." Then she made a glamorous attempt to dust her cigarette ash into the fire.

"I want to be a Mountie. No, maybe I'll drive a tractor-trailer," I said, not knowing then that I would actually drive a truck for two years before going into the furniture business.

"Truck driving's okay, but you can do more than that if you want to. We can do whatever we want to Jimmy. Anything we want!" she said, grabbing my arm and giving it a shake as her eyes widened.

"I suppose, but…"

"It's only a question of what we want to do. Once we figure that out and set our minds to it, we can make it happen. Mom told me that."

"In that case maybe I'll be a space scientist," I said and we both laughed.

Once we were warm again, we climbed the brown-needled crust up the riverbank and followed rabbit tracks, exaggerated from the rain, to a closed-up cottage. There on the veranda, on an old canvas cot, we kissed again, this time with exploring hands rambunctious against winter layers, bringing a clear sense of the sin my mother had been warning me about. Oxhana held her knees tight together, and I respected her judgement. But even at age twelve, I knew I had to try to explore that forbidden territory. She pulled my hand away and slapped it more than once, which was what I expected and was grateful for.

Later, experiencing a feeling between desire and rejection, I gave her the onyx ring my grandmother had bought for me at Peoples Credit Jewellers for ten dollars. We hugged before going to our separate sides of the river. Yes, I gave Oxhana Hlodan my ring on the veranda of that cottage on Taylors Mountain the winter I was twelve. I awoke the next morning happy and excited about going to school because I knew she would be there.

While in my mind, that day had made her my true friend forever, we never really dated. She didn't invite me to her senior prom. Instead she asked my older brother Paul because he was driving my father's car by then. Of course, I felt rejected. I spent that early summer prom night drifting on the river, not thinking of Oxhana exactly but planning my next move that would follow in a series of moves which would take me away from the river altogether. It was as if I knew that someday if things went sour for her, she would return to our remote little world to share it and all its simplicity with me. Even though she had returned my ring within a week.

Later that summer, on a Sunday in August, at the time my mother called "dog days," I ran into Oxhana at the shore. For something to do we drifted down the river in her father's old plywood boat. This time she had brought the cigarettes, and while she reclined on the warm boards in front of me and smoked, I stood in the stern and poled, trying to keep from staring at her pretty bare legs. In a place where the water was very deep I lost my balance and fell overboard. Although I could swim, I was disoriented from the impact and was struggling to get turned around. Then Oxhana was there beside me, reaching for my hand like a ghost through a heavy fog. Her hair was floating around her face like undulating strands of eelgrass and her sleek body moved in the water, curving and dipping like she was a mermaid. We clutched each other and swam back to the boat. Oxhana would help me like that, but would seldom accept my help in return. She was independent that way.

Sometimes on the way home from school, she stopped at our house to sing while Paul played the piano. It seemed she was always preparing for some school concert or talent show that was coming to the village. I did not go to see Oxhana in the talent contest she had entered that August. They had built a stage outdoors for the contestants, and folks sat on canvas chairs or on the grass to listen to them sing and be interviewed by the school principal from town. My brother played guitar for Oxhana. He told me afterwards that she had not sung well. She had tried to talk in a voice not her own, plus she had painted herself up to look less beautiful than she really was. The old men judges had ogled her, but she didn't win a prize.

Later that same year Oxhana and I spent a day gathering Christmas trees from her father's woods. In the evening we loaded the trees on Mr. Hlodan's pickup to take them to the village to sell. We were trying to earn enough money to get us into a dance. As I drove along the gravel road, Oxhana sat on the top of the load to hold down the trees. Near Lockstead, a wheel went into a hole and the load swayed, knocking her over the side so that she fell almost under a moving wheel. She landed face-first into the gravel. When I reached the village and discovered that she wasn't with me, I hurried back to look for her. She was limping along, rubbing her back, a tiny tree in her hand. She was okay but she had broken off her front tooth, which ruined her otherwise perfect smile.

When Oxhana's father died from diabetes in June 1962, he was laid out at the Hlodan house. I went across the river to the wake. The whole community was there; men were standing about the dooryard looking awkward in their dress clothes, rolling cigarettes and talking in murmurs, while the women sat in the parlour by the remains, to be a comfort to Mrs. Hlodan. I had not intended to go into the house, but when Oxhana came out to have a smoke (wearing her white sundress and leather sandals) she took my hand.

"Jimmy, you must come way in and see Daddy!"

At nineteen, I still had not seen a dead person. I nervously followed her through the crowded porch and the more crowded kitchen into the parlour where the gauze curtains had been drawn and the lamp cast a pink glow on the wallpaper. The smell of cut flowers was pink, like the lilacs by the door, and thick as ether. Harry was laying in his grey suit, in a grey casket. Without his glasses, his face appeared to be painted, like the plaster of Paris angels we had made at vacation bible school. I thought I was going to be sick. Oxhana held my hand as we looked at her father. I felt the presence of everyone in the room who came and whispered, "I'm sorry for your troubles," and shook her hand.

"I think he looks really nice," she said to me, "considering what he's been through. Don't you?" I agreed, even though I didn't think he looked nice at all. Now when I attend a wake, I think of that evening at the Hlodan house and I see Harry. And Oxhana is there beside me.

It was probably two years before I saw Oxhana again. This time we were on Spring Garden Road in Halifax in an early summer of the mid-sixties. She was wearing shorts and a halter top and in her bare feet. Her running shoes were tied by the laces to her belt. She was very dark and had a red headband holding down her hair. There was a small tattoo on the biceps of each arm and one on the outside of her right thigh. Had I not seen her broken tooth, I would not have recognized her. She bent over, tossing her hair from side to side, then she wandered into the street, impeding traffic and giving the finger to drivers who honked or whistled. With her was a bearded man in denim clothing. He was sitting on a motorcycle, and, as I approached, the odour of stale sweat and marijuana mixed with the gasoline to make an unfamiliar sweet smell. I waved my arms and shouted to her, but she only gave me a glance and kept on with what she was doing, as if she was understanding things I could never possibly learn, as if hers had become a world I should never really know. Even now, I believe my greatest wisdom is the knowledge that I do not know about such things and can never really fit into certain packages.

I never saw Oxhana again. I had heard that she married a military man who was said to be a drinker and a scrapper and that they had moved overseas. I wondered about her off and on until she eventually faded from my conscious life.

I have assembled the facts, gradually. Oxhana Hlodan had indeed married a man from Halifax and together they'd had two children before things went sour. They divorced and she had stayed single while raising and educating her two daughters, Amanda and Heather, who I am told look exactly like their mother. Then Oxhana met a gentleman from the Canadian Embassy in India and lived in a stately old home in the city of Mangalore. Amanda became a teacher. Heather was studying medicine, and she was on duty at the big hospital in Coimbatore when the ambulance arrived with her mother, who was already dead. Oxhana had collapsed on the sidewalk on her way to work at the elementary school where she had taught for years.

It seems that since Oxhana's and my school days together, someone has cranked up the clock and all of the seasons of our adult lives have slid past like days and nights. The events of long ago have either become buried and forgotten or are confined to a sacred place to be relived. It is said that how we see our childhood, the picture of our youth, is what counts most since that is the mythology from which we invent ourselves. Oxhana Hlodan pursued and captured her dream, keeping the image of her higher self alive while working to achieve it. I think of this often, and how she would build me up when I was down. *We can do whatever we want to do Jimmy! It's just a matter of perception.* I had leaned on her for support. And many times since I have looked to her for encouragement.

Still, I have long since come to believe that life can never be the way we perceived it from our youth. There is always a new way of thinking, and we have to be able to adapt. I have grasped for cherries on boughs beyond my reach. Those cherries grew into plums and then apples, which were completely out of my grasp. Along the way I have looked for the missing pieces to assemble the jigsaw puzzle of my life, to make the picture right. Yet all the dreams began to fade and I subconsciously agreed to let them go. In a sense, all of the helping hands, the props, and the bonfires of my youth had turned to smouldering heaps of grey ash. Mythologies have been traded for priorities and my music has grown out of date. And all the philosophers and teachers in the world cannot put the picture back together, not the way it was.

Now, from out of the wind or a the lyrics of an old country song, you appear. I can scent your perfume, hear your ragged voice. You beckon, and we return to that time and place which has to do only with you and me. You are there beside me in that foreboding country schoolhouse, steadfast and mature, with a helping hand, the same young Oxhana Hlodan, pretty but obscure. Sometimes, too, we meet in your old wainscot kitchen and I watch you put on your mother's makeup. Then we share that first kiss, again. We talk in the country accent we all had but couldn't hear. Then we slip away to the river and skate, letting ourselves move in unison, unbound and free, reliving our dreams as we make moving shadows on the pond.

SUMMER

The Raft

There was a vacated mill yard on the riverbank a few kilometres above my home. It was scattered with dry cedar logs, which had been rejected from the mill. Some of these were kinked; others had hollow ends and red rot. The bark had fallen from them so they were smooth and orange coloured. Harold Camp and I carried a dozen of these to the shore in back of Bergans Island, where there was an eddy and a flat piece of gravel beach. With the axe and saw and a bag of spikes we built a raft, which we named *April*, while Oxhana Hlodan ran about collecting pieces of plywood to make a shelter on one end. The board she salvaged was decayed black like the framework of the abandoned mill so our raft which took us three days to complete, resembled a cook scow for a log driving crew.

We launched *April* by breaking a bottle of 7Up against the corner of its shack. Then we got on the raft and with poles pushed her adrift. This was the day we would drift down the river fifteen kilometres to Quarryville. It was Saturday morning, July 4, 1960. Oxhana had just graduated from high school. It was her last year of hanging out on the river with Harold and me. Everyone in our community wished her well.

On this morning there was plenty of water for good rafting, but we struggled to get *April* out into the heavy water with the poles. Oxhana's mother had packed us a lunch, and Harold had brought a fishing rod and his old guitar. The river was quite high for so late in the season and for the first few kilometres, Oxhana and I stood at the rear and steered. Harold sat on a bench in the shelter, strummed his guitar *I got my connections on the fourth day of July. The train being late or my being too soon...* It was a song about a prostitute, the only one I ever heard him sing. Harold looked like Willie Nelson with the long hair and headband. Even now when I hear that old song I think of rafting the summer that Oxhana and I were seventeen, and Harold was eighteen.

We kept in the middle of the river, which was smooth and fast. The water had a sparkle in it because of the breeze. The sky was clear, the sun hot. Occasionally, a salmon jumped or a sea run trout or shad splashed. I cast for these, and once I hooked a big brookie. We pulled it onto the raft and killed it to cook later that day. As we drifted, several motorboats passed so close the waves lapped over our outside logs. These were river guides, who shouted to us to keep our comic book shack adrift. As the water dripped from our poles to wet our pant legs, the amber gravel beneath us receded fast toward the rear of the raft.

Long before we got to the village of Blackville we steered *April* into an eddy at the foot of an island called Washburns, and there we built a fire to make tea and roast the trout. We reclined in the sun, much warmer on the shore. It was too early in the summer for the flies to bother us. Toads sang along the river as we ate our meal and looked about the side hill for wood to keep the fire going. Oxhana came back to the raft with a bouquet of violets.

Later, after Harold had built up the fire, an upriver breeze got into the blaze and it caught the dead grass, spreading quickly across the elm-treed island. In a panic we took off our jackets and tried to beat out the flame, which gained momentum across the dusty interval. A white smoke billowed up the river. Oxhana was so engrossed in fighting the blaze that the hem of her blue jeans caught fire. She had to run to the water and wade in to save her pants from burning. The fire eventually burned itself out, leaving Harold and I black-faced and sweating and Oxhana in charred pants. She went into the trees then, took off her jeans and with the axe made them into a pair of shorts with frayed and jagged bottoms, the kind we saw in cartoons. It was the first time I had seen real cut-offs in the making.

Then we were back on the raft and moodily drifting around the Golden Horseshoe, past Taylors Mountain and through Bulls Run, down under the wire bridge at home, toward the village. Along the way, Harold stabbed at the bottom with the pole, trying to steer us away from shallow bars and submerged boulders that made wakes. By this time Oxhana was sitting in the shelter, bare foot. Her white legs were covered in goosebumps from the breeze even though it was a hot day for the time of year. It is always cooler on the river. She put my coat around her and took her turn on the guitar singing, "Beautiful, beautiful brown eyes…" Her husky young voice carried on the water for a long way. She could really sing that song, Oxhana could.

In Blackville we drifted to shore at the mouth of Bartholomew River and tied the raft to a tree. We walked up the hill to Geo's canteen. In the village it was like midsummer. Store doors were propped open, and people were mowing their lawns. The scent of new-cut grass was in the wind. Geraniums were blooming in window boxes.

There were no customers in the restaurant as we sat on stools at the bar and ordered colas from the waiter. Harold bought a pack of Export As, which we shared while plugging nickels into the dome-top jukebox. We listened to Del Shannon, Ricky Nelson, and Elvis. When two older women came in, they looked at Oxhana's bare feet and legs.

"Well good God, what will they be wearing next?" the older one said.

"And with two young men. They're so bold nowadays," said the other woman.

"She's smoking. We wonder why they get into trouble so young."

As we were leaving we heard the older woman say, "I wonder if her mother knows where she is?"

Then we were drifting again, out into the heavier currents. We worried about the rapids ahead and wondered if our raft would hold together. The Gray, Black, and White Rapids were around the bend, and all of these had plenty of boulders and shallows where the river was scattered and strong enough to grind a raft into splinters. Or maybe the water would push us between boulders and leave us wedged there. We knew, too, that if we hit a blind rock in midstream where the water was strong we would capsize. But there was great excitement in the fear that lived in us as we approached this dangerous stretch.

The river is big and rugged near the head of tide. There would be no houses visible from shore, as the banks are protected by a steep, treed ledge. We talked about how the Miramichi was like two different rivers, the turbulent one below the village and the smooth and slow one above with the elm trees and the strawlike grassy shores.

We had drifted for almost an hour without any obstructions. Through the Gray Rapids, past Liars Rock, and the long gravel beach underwater. Through the Black Rapids we had kept close to the south side, smooth sailing. But we were mostly quiet because of our unease about what lay just ahead. In the distance we could see and hear the White Rapids, a frothing, gulping stretch of swift water. There was a big brook, pouring over a ledge, its white water descending into the main river and making a foam line on the surface. We spied an abandoned cabin on a high bluff. From here the river tumbled over ledges like a long and spiralled set of stairs, and we could see rooster tails of white water and hear the frightening freshet sounds. Why had we decided to do this anyway? And where exactly would be the right place to go through the first set of rapids? We knew people had drowned trying to come up the right side with motorboats early in the spring.

It was too late to change course. We were unable to steer because the strong water had pretty much given our raft a mind of its own.

As Harold poked the bottom and desperately pried against the logs to keep in the channel, the raft swung onto his pole and snapped it out of his hand. It went under and was gone. With only the small pole left, we knew we were at the mercy of the water and the raft's durability, which was already starting to creak. We pledged to stay with it whatever happened, to hang together. We were looking for a shallow place where we might jump clear and wade to shore. There was only the amber bottom, well down, quickly receding beneath us.

The raft twisted off boulders and dropped its outside logs under the currents. We hung on to each other in the little shanty. I began to panic like I used to when I woke up with an asthma attack in the middle of the night. And I swore that I had dreamed all of this before.

"Jimmy you're as white as a ghost!" Oxhana said to me.

"I'm okay, I think. But I can't swim much and…"

"Just hang on. Whatever happens, hang on!" Oxhana Hlodan was prying sideways with the pole. Suddenly the raft stopped completely. We were jammed between some boulders. The logs shuddered and creaked as the currents tugged at the edges of the raft, the water around us too swift and deep to stand in. Then we were lifting, lifting on the upriver end and our shelter was going under. We ran to the other end. Howard staggered and slipped overboard. He tried to hang on to the outside log but was getting pulled under.

"Hang on! For God's sake, hang on to the log," Oxhana cried above the rushing of the water. "Jimmy, get over here."

I could not breathe. Oxhana tried to grasp Harold's flailing hands, but he was already somewhere beneath us. I clung to the shack and could see short images from my life: school days, building the raft, and now death by drowning. But I had a lot of faith in Oxhana Hlodan. And I had a lot of faith in Harold. I had seen them in the river so many times. Still, Harold was down a good long time. I imagined myself having to tell his parents he had drowned.

I whimpered, "Oh God where is he!"

"Jimmy please!"

"Hang on!"

"No, you hang on. Keep cool, I'm okay!"

How could I tell Oxhana's folks if something happened to her? Our parents would never have approved of this raft trip. So we had not told them. Now brief nightmares flashed and were gone, flashed and were gone.

Harold seemed to be under for minutes but it was only seconds, the way time passes with panic. His head surfaced downstream and he was making overhand strokes, desperately, like Ophelia with a change of heart. My head was aching. Even though we were not yet out of danger, Oxhana and I relaxed. We gave out a reckless laugh at the sight of Harold dog paddling. Because he was the oldest, we had put our trust in him. With Harold it was all danger and drowning one minute and safely reliving the incident the next, the way that near-catastrophes sometimes go. When he reached shore he stood on a rock, shivering and coughing as he tried to tell us to jump clear and head for shore before we were also swept under.

Oxhana took my hand and together we jumped. The cold water, which moved like a conveyer belt under us, took my breath away. Oxhana half-waded half-fell in a clumsy fray, dragging the two of us towards the shore, gritting her teeth, grunting angrily, and crying the whole way.

"C'mon Oxy! C'mon Oxy, you can do it," Howard shouted. The squirrels and the birds scampered about in the trees, which were sighing with concern.

We sloshed onto the rocks and stood together, hugging and trembling and crying as the raft broke in half. The two pieces let go from the rocks to drift around the bend out of sight, Harold's guitar propped upright in the shanty. We never saw it again.

We went into the trees and took off our clothes. We wrung them out as best we could and put them back on, still dripping. Then we headed toward the highway, where we could hitchhike home.

The Chambermaid's Daughter

Her mother had never wanted Beatrice to go and would miss her help. But Bee knew that leaving home would lighten her father's load. Charlie McKnight, who had never been able to keep a steady job, was supporting his family of eleven with just two boys to help him on the farm. That his second eldest daughter was the best worker, even in the fields and barns, never seemed to matter. To become a favourite around home, she would have to work harder than her sisters and brothers. Bee might have been a boy herself. At age sixteen it was obvious she would never be pretty. She was slim with a big square face and a homely smile. Her threat of leaving had been a joke at first, maybe a plea for acceptance. However it was, she built on a near smile, a sigh, or even a twinkle in his eye from her father when she first mentioned going away. Beatrice felt she would be thought more of for relieving her father of a mouth to feed. Better to be popular for leaving young than to remain a homebody and a burden. She would make a living on her own, if only across the river.

"She'll be back before the summer's over!" her older sister Maude said. Overhearing this, Beatrice became even more determined to leave and stay away longer. She left home with her family's blessing and not much more. She carried a small bag of belongings, among them a new apron her mother had given her as a parting gift. She left in her bare feet, for it was the summer of 1942, not long after the Great Depression, and there was no money for such luxuries as shoes. But she was not going far. The Wentworths would certainly know that she had nothing to bring.

Beatrice McKnight would go to work for the Wentworth family as a chambermaid, just as her mother had done years before at a home in town. Alice Wentworth had four frail sons and an oversize neglected house. She needed a maid. Her husband Frank, who owned the river boom company, was seldom home and had no attraction to his house and family. They would pay Beatrice fifty cents a day for scrubbing floors, washing clothes, making beds, cooking, and looking after the children. In her spare time she would tend the vegetable garden.

They gave Beatrice a room in the attic, which was accessible only from out back in the summer kitchen. When she wasn't working, Bee stayed mostly in her room, reading or knitting, especially if Alice Wentworth had company. In the off hours Beatrice would escape down the back kitchen stairs and take a walk to the fields or the river. She needed this to clear her head from the Wentworth way of things, which at times seemed to overwhelm her. In the back field she would sit on a flat rock and stare across the river valley, try to contemplate her future, which seemed to hold only small pockets of hope, distorted like help signals out of a storm.

No one really knew just how lonely Beatrice McKnight was in that first summer away from her home, even though she had been bereft of love and overworked there, too. She had never enjoyed usual girlhood experiences, nor had she attended school, though she could read and write. It seemed she had been born for hardship, had gone from childhood to womanhood overnight. Still, aching from too much labour and lonesome as she was, Beatrice had more freedom at the Wentworth farm than she ever did at home, and life was somewhat easier because this family, especially Frank Wentworth, was kind to her and they were not so poor.

But freedom was not what Beatrice McKnight craved most. It was love. She was a prisoner of poverty, but she was also deprived of the friendships and camaraderie, even the lovesickness that a youth her age should experience. There were no other teenagers outside of her family in Barnettville. Especially on weekends, Beatrice wandered the fields and river valley of the Wentworth's farm, lonely and lost.

Frank was the first to notice. He was subtle about things like love, and on the outside no one suspected that he, too, longed for it. He began to meet Beatrice in a field, quite casually at first, when she had gone to the back pasture to fetch the cows. Later he would hide in the trees with a little cow bell to lure her there. They would sit and talk. Soon she was waiting for him. He would appear from out of the trees to sit beside her and gently hold her hand, callused and faded already from her labour. Each of them seemed to be able to tell what the other was thinking. In their brief eye contact they both felt a burning passion that neither had experienced before. It set Beatrice's heart pounding and she would blush and giggle. Frank Wentworth, remaining cool on the surface, became fevered inside. He could see in the young woman a kind of desperation, and it occurred to him that she could become his for the taking. She found Frank Wentworth tremendously handsome; he found Beatrice McKnight very lonely.

At first Frank would only hug her briefly and be gently pushed away. Eventually, she let him soothe and cradle her in his arms.

"For all you know Bee, I could be in love with you already!" he chuckled one evening as he stroked her long hair.

Beatrice grinned and squeezed his hands. She felt this way too, though she couldn't say it. As fleeting as their meetings were, Beatrice regarded them as something to build on and the most important experiences of her life. Even though she knew she was much younger, she did not feel deceived by him, rather absorbed. It was as though they had been two distant fuses ignited long ago to burn now toward the same end, an end which Beatrice had experienced only in dreams. She had been released from the frustrations and neglect that had brought her here, and this overshadowed any shame that loving Frank Wentworth could bring.

As they strolled one afternoon to their usual spot, Beatrice decided she would give herself to him, there beneath the pine trees in the tall grass along the riverbank. She envisioned the moment even as they walked. Beatrice McKnight had not planned her life this way. She had dreamed of her first time in a feathered bed with a young sea captain from the Royal Reserve whose photograph she had cut out of a magazine and whose image she had carried with her through those restless nights following adolescence.

Now, as Beatrice and Frank lay together sweating in their heated movements and their own desires that were also fears, the birds and small animals and the trees stopped to watch. Beatrice sensed that she had conceded to Frank too soon, but this she buried quickly for the pleasures of the moment. Still, this flash of wisdom had shot through her, triggered perhaps from her mother's warnings, the voice of conscience from a woman whose house Beatrice could see on the other side of the river. She was that close to home. But Bee's desires were stronger than conscience or anything else that her mother had warned her about. Life could not be *that* simple.

"Oh Frank, I will always be faithful to you." she whispered afterwards as they stood and embraced. "You know I'll never let you down!"

Even though Frank had been overcome with passion for his teenaged chambermaid only minutes before, now he only smiled.

"Shhh," he said softly as he laid a finger on her lips. He had slept with her, yes, but feeling a touch of guilt he wondered if it should ever happen again. When he looked into Beatrice's moist eyes, he could see that she had read things differently.

Already it was love for Beatrice, a secret one, even though she felt sometimes like the world should know and share her new feelings; they were that strong. Of course, this could never be. It was not that simple; life was never simple for a McKnight. Frank Wentworth was someone else's husband, a respectable businessman, a pillar of the community. Beatrice McKnight was his chambermaid, someone from the other side of the river. This station she would not outgrow, not in one generation or even two. Alice Wentworth would certainly never let her forget that. Yet this was the first time in her life that Beatrice felt wanted. Though she knew that to love in this way was a disgrace and a sin, she did not feel guilty because there was something about Alice Wentworth that she never really understood, or wanted to. Was it jealously? Deceit?

Often Alice would push Beatrice to do more than she could, then scold her if she failed. Other times Alice would be overly nice. When there was a social function at the school or church, Alice would go, leaving Beatrice in charge of the house. This gave Beatrice a small sense of pride, even though she knew that if Alice Wentworth was aware it was picking her up she wouldn't have done so—she preferred making things harder. Once in a while Mrs. Wentworth would take a train trip to Halifax and be away for days. During these stints away, Beatrice would put on the jewellery that Frank had bought for Alice while she prepared his meal or ironed his clothes. She also wore the pretty new apron that her mother had given her.

At first Alice would bring home gifts for Beatrice, just like she did the family. But after she found out that her teenaged chambermaid was pregnant, she never went anywhere or allowed Beatrice out of her sight. While Alice Wentworth claimed that she never really knew who the baby's father was (and Beatrice could never tell), Frank's household name had become Frank-you-son-of-a-bitch. But they all agreed that, to spare the Wentworth home a scandal, the chambermaid's pregnancy should be kept hidden from the McKnights and indeed the community. Beatrice would not go home now until after the birth. The baby would be raised as a Wentworth from the maid's quarters in the attic, even though it would arrive long after Alice Wentworth's child-bearing years. Beatrice might have left with the baby had it not been for Frank, and so might have Alice, had she another place to go.

By now Beatrice could see herself becoming a secret part of Frank Wentworth's family. If only Alice weren't in the picture, she thought. Maybe the old hag will leave someday. She had an image of her and Frank sharing his house with comfort, employing a maid themselves. They would raise a large family, travel, take in church and school socials together. Of course, this was still a long way off. Beatrice knew that if she and the baby could be here with Frank, even part-time, it would be enough for the present. She cherished her moments with him despite knowing that Frank's wife was still in the picture.

Frank Wentworth carried a vision of his own, a sketchy, almost inaccessible image of things the way he would have them. The image certainly did not include Alice. But Beatrice was not exactly a part of it either, not yet. If she were, it would certainly not be out of obligation. There had been no bargaining. The situation would all come together in time if it was meant to, if something grew in that direction of its own accord. He would move slowly and observe.

Alice was becoming more vexing by the day. As Beatrice carried the heavy scrub buckets, tended to the cultivating, ironed and cooked, Alice constantly chastised her for leaving chores half done: a dangerous wet floor, a wrinkled sheet, a wasted burnt crust of bread. Once, during a meal when Frank was away, Alice threw a table knife at Beatrice for overcooking the meat.

Beatrice began having a recurring dream of pushing her employer through an upstairs window to a stubborn suicide. There were times in conversation with Alice when Bee had raised the axe but didn't drop it. She could have told her a few things, thrown fuel onto smouldering ashes. But she said nothing. Instead Beatrice would find some consolation in Frank's impending return, coming home from business travels for Christmas, if not Thanksgiving, to make suffering the abuse worthwhile. She would be spending the holidays at the Wentworth home this year. If things went right she could steal away to the woods with Frank, for a tree. They could do this as long as Frank said so, even if Alice objected. Beatrice also knew that her unfulfilled dreams were in the delicate nurturing stage. She would have to stay out of sight and wait if she was going to help Frank keep peace. For a long time she had feared what Alice might do, and more or less stayed in the attic. Beatrice knew she would have to rely on Frank's support, however subtle. So she suffered alone, knowing that even now with the baby's coming, the pain was worth enduring, more so than any hurt she had ever experienced.

A baby girl was born in the maid's quarters on a cold day in the dead of winter with only a midwife to help. The child was scrawny with black wiry hair like the McKnights, instead of red like the Wentworths. She was nursed on her mother's breast, even as the young chambermaid carried out her household duties. The chores had been increased (out of spite), and the work continually fell short of Alice Wentworth's satisfaction. It was impossible. Beatrice could do nothing right. In the spring, while Bee was nursing her daughter, Alice had come in to demand that she hoe the kitchen garden before it was completely overrun by wildflowers.

"I'll do it! When there's time, I'll do it Mrs. Wentworth, " Bee had said.

"Oh you'll do it! You'll do it, by Jesus. I guess we all know that much about you now and just what you, will do!" Alice retorted sarcastically.

The next morning Beatrice overheard Alice talking to her husband at the breakfast table. "I want her out of this house today, the slut! Either she goes, or I go."

"No Alice, Bee has to stay, at least for now," Frank said. "And the baby stays. Where else can she go? She can't take the baby away from here! She can't go home. How could we explain that? And we can't expect her to leave it behind." As Frank spoke it seemed he could have cared less about what his wife thought.

"No, we certainly don't want it left here," Alice scoffed.

One evening Alice tiptoed down the stairs to overhear broken whispers from the dining room. "Frank, I want you to help me name the baby!" Beatrice was pleading. "Do you like the name Vivian?"

Alice quietly slipped away before Frank could respond, as though she were accepting the situation, at least momentarily, or she had a sudden impulse not to care. Alice kept her nose in the air and contributed nothing to running the household. She shivered and frowned at the smallest whimper from the baby. Sometimes she would play the piano with vigour to drown out Vivian's crying, or perhaps to make the baby cry louder. Beatrice couldn't tell.

Vivian was not a well child and cried a lot. She had big dark eyes, which were slanted slightly, and her mother's cheekbones, which Alice envied. She was exceptionally homely because of her freckles and teeth that would obviously protrude, making her the object of derision from the Wentworth boys. Alice Wentworth, seemed to be blushing all the time now behind her wire-rimmed spectacles and shunning Beatrice and Vivian, especially in the company of her relatives from Lockstead.

As Vivian grew, she took in stride the mockery from her "siblings" as if it were normal or even a kind of compliment. She liked the attention. She was incapable of dishonesty herself and loved them all. To win attention she tried to be funny. She would put on an old pair of Alice's high-heel shoes, a bonnet, and shawl, pucker her little face and suck in her cheeks to make her teeth protrude even more. This expression along with her spindly legs above the large shoes made her look like a strange large bird. Vivian would cackle like a beggar and be witty and full of life. She could mimic anyone, and she liked to sing in her raspy little voice.

At these performances Beatrice's eyes would light up and she would muse in a near smile, trying to divert the attention of the household to her daughter. Frank would look at Vivian, then at Beatrice, and laugh. Vivian would have talent. Anyone could see that. But because she was so delicate, she had not started school by age six. The only education she received was from Beatrice, who had taught her the alphabet, how to count, and tell time. And she liked to listen to the stories Beatrice told her.

It seemed that Beatrice was always trying to protect Vivian from scorn. In the off hours, they would escape together. Bee would carry Vivian in a makeshift harness on her back to the river, stepping through fields of wildflowers, the wind in their dark hair. They picked berries and sometimes sampled the wild apples from a tree at the back of the pasture. Once in a while Beatrice would make a strawberry-flavoured gelatine, which they cooled in the spring beside the trays of milk and cream. Vivian would gorge on the treat and giggle, hugging her mother's legs. The more Beatrice made of her, the more her daughter grinned and hugged her.

Vivian was old enough now that Beatrice was able to leave her and go home to visit her mother occasionally. One evening Bee was at home helping her mother rearrange furniture in the stairs. She glanced across the river through the early dusk to the Wentworth's and saw a lamp burning in their spare bedroom. She called her mother to the window and they both wondered at the neighbours having this room open so late in the autumn. It looked as if someone had trimmed the lamp and the room had become very bright. Then it dimmed and went out completely. Neither of them had ever known that room to be used except in summer, when relatives came.

The next morning when Beatrice went to work, she asked Mrs. Wentworth about the lighted room. Alice told her that no one had been in the spare room the night before. It must have been the full moon reflecting off the water, which had been known to light up the window that way. Or perhaps the whole thing was another one of Beatrice's illusions.

The following afternoon Vivian fell ill with whooping cough, which put a great strain on Beatrice.

"It's your child, so you look after it!" Alice said.

On her hands and knees, Beatrice scrubbed Vivian's room, as well as the rest of the house. Then she burned sulphur throughout the stairs to kill the germs. She bathed and rocked her child, day and night, with no help from anyone, told her little yarns, and brought her hot broth. Vivian whooped and coughed and gagged to her half-brothers' amusement. Even as she grew weak and according to the doctor, very susceptible to the influenza, she tried to be funny. Everyone thought that little Vivian had a great spirit to joke about something as torturous as whooping cough. But Alice said nothing.

Vivian had not fully recovered and was still weak, when she became ill again. This time she did not try to be funny but lay sleeping. Again the doctor was called to the Wentworth house even though Alice had warned they could not afford more doctor bills. This time Dr. Beaton folded his spectacles, looked down at the floor and shook his head. As far as he could see Vivian had contracted pneumonia and there wasn't much that he could do. Beatrice moved her child into the spare room to care for her there. The doctor removed the window glass and told Mrs. Wentworth to make sure it was left out because the child needed fresh air. If she worsened he was to be called at once. In bed, Vivian cried and picked the patch quilt with her little index finger as her mother nervously tended to her, while in the hallway Frank Wentworth paced, the picture of despair.

"Bee, tell me a story," Vivian kept saying, as if the telling would return things to what they had been when she was well. Beatrice sat tirelessly in the sickroom, concentrating to make the little stories more animated, tales of little girls in Sunday dresses, romping through fields to catch butterflies or wandering with playmates by the shore to look at their reflections in the water. For Vivian the continuous sound of her mother's voice was more comforting than the stories. Distorted as it was, it took Vivian's thoughts away from her illness. The young chambermaid talked on into the nights, repeating the stories anew. If she left the room even briefly, Vivian cried, so Beatrice slept on a quilt folded upon four chairs pushed together beside her daughter's bed.

In the morning Beatrice went downstairs for something to eat. When she returned, she sat on the bed and took the child's little hand. It was on fire. Vivian was craving an apple, so Beatrice hurried to the back pasture to pick one from the wild tree. When she gave the apple to Vivian, the child took only one bite, quickly laid it aside then almost sat up.

"Bee, you are so good to me!" she said and she put her little arms around Beatrice's neck and held her tight. When Beatrice laid her back on the pillow there was a smile on her face.

"Vivian dear, you look just like a little angel laying there, you're so pretty," she said. Vivian smiled again and appeared very content and happy. Then she shivered and twitched beneath the covers and drifted away. Away and away and away, until she stopped breathing and the smile started to grow cold and stiff. Dark-eyed Vivian's plaited black hair lay upon the pillow around her. Beatrice went to the window and took a wildflower from the vase. She tucked it in her daughter's hair and adjusted the bed clothes neatly around her. With her delicate frame there in the bed and her wiry hair softened by the white flower, everyone in the house—even Alice when she came to the room—had to agree that Vivian looked just like a little angel.

Through the morning, Beatrice waited in the bedroom with its grievous smells of chamber pot slop and burning sulphur to wait for the undertaker. When he arrived, she helped him put Vivian in her Sunday dress and tried to hide her protruding teeth. They laid her in a little white casket and fixed her hair nicely with the flower in it, but her face was white as cotton. They carried her down the stairs and into the Wentworth's front parlour to be waked. As Beatrice stood beside the child's coffin, clutching the apple that Vivian had so recently made tiny tooth marks in, everyone in the community came to see and to shake hands with the Wentworths and ask if there was anything at all that they could do. Everyone remarked that Vivian was a very pretty little girl, though her face was now like wax.

It was only then that things seemed to close in around Beatrice, darken and close in like converging paths in a forest. She was feeling the reality of being alone now, confused and lost, secretly grieving the loss of her daughter. Frank was always at the back of her mind. Frank. Would he be there when she needed him?

It was a dark breezy day with black raindrops zigzagging down the coach windows as they drove Vivian's casket to the churchyard. They buried her just inside the ornate wrought-iron fence of the Wentworth's family plot, beneath the yellow leaves of October. As the old words were being read, *O grave, where is thy victory?*, Frank Wentworth briefly left his wife's side for all to see, to go over and embrace his grieving chambermaid, standing silently beside their daughter's grave. Only then did Beatrice, knowing that she was alone in this now, wonder where he had been. For a moment anger mixed with sorrow. She could have let the axe drop again.

Beatrice McKnight's loneliness resigned again to loneliness itself, to build in solitude once more from nothing. Her hunger had been discovered, fed and even nourished for a time. But all too soon it had smothered and died like a wildflower laid to waste when its stem has broken in a storm. To be discarded now by Frank Wentworth like an apple fallen prematurely from a wild tree and left, worthless, to decay before the frost that honeycombs the autumn sand had turned to snow and she could claim the hand that might have made it go. She had almost grasped life.

After the funeral, Beatrice went home to be with her family. She walked the short piece of highway, crossed the river in the Wentworth's canoe, headed down the shore in her bare feet, just as she had done years before when she left home. Feeling a new world of emptiness now, she sat in the rain on the veranda steps of her mother's house and cried. Had any of it been real?

Her mother came out of the house to sit on the step above her daughter and put her hand on Beatrice's shoulder. She told Beatrice that she should not cry about other people's troubles; it would come home to haunt them if she grieved too much about someone who was not really family. After all, everything that she had done for the Wentworths was just part of a chambermaid's job.

Beatrice McKnight sat on the veranda step, her mother above her, the rain coming down.

"Aaahhh, but it's no use though Minnie. I don't think there is a fish in the river if ya wanna know the truth of it." Willie was talking to his mother as he looked about the shed and the dooryard for his old fishing tackle. "But I s'pose I'll have ta give 'er a try. Ya say ya wanna piece a fish fer tomorrow."

"Yes I would like a piece a fish. Good God, I never saw a man fish so many hours and bring nothin' home."

"It's not the fish I go after Minnie, ya must know that. It's the fun a fishin'."

"Well maybe you'd get us a fish this time, just fer the fun of it. I sure would like a fish fer the table."

She always asked him to catch one when Sara and Tim were coming home from the city for the weekend. They would be here tomorrow. He hadn't asked but he knew by the pressure she had put on him that they were coming. He would have to take a back seat again, until they left.

Willie had always wished that he could have been like his older brother, Tim, to be Minnie's favourite son so she would bring home gifts for him when she went on trips. The gifts had always been for Tim and their sister Sara—the popular children. Willie felt that this was because he had quit school, had not been able to handle the pressures of the classroom. Yet he knew he was able to do some things right because he was the one she relied on to bring home the fish.

"I'll see what I can do fer ya. But, ya know I gave up fishin' back a spell. I gave it up fer bingo. I figured me chances were better in the public hall than out there on the river."

"Well, I'd have to agree with you there."

"There's not many fish in the river nowadays, not like there used to be. But did ya see that old rod of mine anywhere?"

"Yes I saw yer rod the other day somewhere and I thought, 'well what a waste of money that was.' Oh yes, it was standing out there, behind the backhouse."

Willie stomped around the yard looking like he had developed a certain indifference to the experience. The truth is, he had grown away from fishing and wanted to go to Doaktown, where he could hang out at the convenience store or the big restaurant. But he spotted his rod propped up behind the abandoned outhouse. He picked it up and examined it. It was broken in the middle and repaired with black electrical tape, but when he threaded the line through the guides and gave the rod a bowlike pull, it seemed to bend evenly. He stripped some line off the reel and it squeaked of grit, sounding like an old-fashioned egg beater as he cranked it awkwardly, after making a test cast in the dooryard.

"Aaaaahhh? It's no use Minnie. A man could never land a salmon on that anyway."

"But maybe ya could, too."

Willie sang as he stomped across the hayfields toward the river and the old home pool. His blond hair projected from beneath his baseball cap, his bare arms speckled with pitch from having spent the day working in the woods. It was good to get out of the house, to get away from Minnie's bantering. Why did she always pick on him to do things?

At the shore, half-sunken beneath the overhanging rushes, he found the family's old punt with a paddle and pole afloat inside.

From a ring in the boat's bow extended a long chain to which a huge oblong rock, the anchor, was fixed with haywire.

Willie bailed using the paddle as a shovel before setting the anchor on the bow and coiling the chain neatly around it. Then he pushed the boat adrift and started to pole toward centre stream. The boat skimmed through the current and the choppy water lapped against the hull. He braced himself in the stern and guided the craft among hidden boulders, confident he was an excellent canoeist, if only by his own admission. At centre stream the water became very swift, frothing over rocks and the shallows of a gravel bar. This, he knew, was where the big salmon lay during midsummer.

He pushed the anchor overboard and the chain rattled over the gunwales like a machine gun firing. The boat swung sharply and tipped, almost taking in water.

"That's it now, drown yerself," Willie said as the boat skated and fishtailed until he could make his way to the stern. Crouching, he held on to the gunwales to keep balance. The boat dragged to a halt with a firm tug from the heavy anchor on the gravel bottom, straightened in the current, and hung fast. He carefully stood up and looked about. A boil in the water not thirty feet in front of him would be Papas Rock. "Well ya just never know. There could be a salmon right over there at the rock."

His leader was too short, and when he made the first cast, his fly hook plunked the water like a bullet. So he cast upstream and pulled the fly gently over the deep water behind the rock. It was his favourite fly, an Oriole he had bought the summer before at a small shop in Howards. As the line swung, there was a slight boil behind the fly followed by a wake, until the hook stopped short with a firm pull from the depths and a screech from the rusty reel.

"Bollocks! There he is. He's on," Willie said aloud as he jerked up the rod to set the hook in the fish's mouth. His heart pounded as he watched the wake drift away and felt the fish go to the bottom and hold there.

Willie looked to see if anyone was watching him from the shores, but he was alone. He held the rod up, keeping a strain on the fish. After some time the salmon commenced to swim downstream, making the old reel hammer in its frame.

"Ha *Haah*, hello fer takin' off!" Willie was grinning broadly. Then the fish jumped and Willie saw just how big it was, and he frowned, fearing for his tackle.

Holding the rod with one hand, he hurried to the bow, pulling the anchor at intervals. He headed for shore, keeping a tight line, poling when the fish was streaking away from the boat, and poling harder when the fish was coming his way. At one point he held the rod's cork in his teeth and pushed with both hands, keeping the reel's turning crank away from his jaw. The boat struck the shore with a sudden jolt and Willie skidded on its slippery bottom, half-falling overboard and soaking the seat of his pants.

"There ya go, fall in now and drown yerself," he said as he scrambled to his feet. He moved along the shore, trying to pick up some of the line, but did little better than hold his own going through an entanglement of shrubbery and long shore hay.

"No fish I s'pose. But Jesus, I'd like ta land 'im though. I'd give up fishin' fer good, I think. Well fer this summer anyways." Willie usually talked out loud to himself. He stumbled along the shore and cranked in line.

The fish took refuge in the depths of an eddy. There the water was deep and brown, the bottom muddy. A decaying fish that hung from a protruding branch gave off an unpleasant odour. A scum drifted upstream, and mosquitos swarmed above the water. Stepping around a clump of alder, Willie slipped and fell in to just above his knees.

"That's it, ya could drown yerself with any help at all," he said, but got up and kept going.

The salmon rose to the surface, revealing its broad hunched back. It was an old Cains River hook-bill, a good fifty or sixty pounds, the largest fish that he had ever seen. A kind of panic came over

Willie. He whooped and danced. And he shouted for help. Where were the rest of the lads when he needed them?

"Nowhere to be seen, that's where the Jesus they are," he mumbled. He stared into the water trying to get another glimpse. Then his old rod began to buckle.

"Bollocks! She's not gonna stand 'er boys." Willie wondered what he could do to help support the rod. At the repaired section, the tape was giving out and the rod was bending square.

"That's it, come apart now, ya bamboo bastard! Break when I need ya the most." When the fish gave a head shake, the outer half collapsed and drifted off into the water, carried by the tight line. Willie was left holding only the butt end and the reel.

"Hello, wouldn't break. Well there ya go boys." Willie cranked and swayed the stub with extended arms, straining his eyes to see into the amber water for another glimpse of the fish.

Suddenly the big salmon came toward him. Fast. Willie tried desperately to pick up the slack, but the small reel was not fast enough and he was forced to strip in arm lengths, making a coil of line on the grass beneath his feet. At one point, the fish was so close that he tried to grab its tail and could have almost touched it, had he been a little faster.

"Boys, I almost had ya there, lad." Willie was careful not to tangle the line that was coiled under his feet. "Things are going my way a bit now, finally. If he comes in a bit closer I'll—" But the fish turned again and headed toward centre stream.

"This will be his last run, I think. When he comes back in close, I'll tail 'im."

Willie had a brief image of himself carrying the big salmon up the hill to give to Minnie. It made him feel proud. He would have finally contributed something. He would show her that he could do it. A camaraderie would bloom between them, at last. He would be a kid again just for a moment, and this time *he* would be his mother's favourite.

Minnie did not seem to realize that at age forty-two there was still time for him to swing things around. That is, if he could finally get his say in things. He could make the farm bigger and better instead of letting the place go to pieces the way he knew it would after it fell into the hands of his brother and sister. They had taken over their mother's thinking, swung her around so that God only knew what she had put in the will. What troubled him most is that he knew they would have the gall to ask him to help them with its keeping.

"Life!" He gave the salmon play now by fumbling to keep the line free of tangles. Then, as if a fish would know this could happen (or as if something that had always worked against him knew), a root sprang up and clutched the line. It held and held, until it sang like a cello string, cutting Willie's finger to the bone and provoking him into fits of profanity as he tried frantically to untangle it.

"That's it, tangle on me, ya son-of-a-whore. Life is not hard enough without a tangle today."

He could see it all, before it happened. He could see it again, the way life always turned against him. The line snapped. It hit the water like an elastic band and vanished.

The salmon jumped. Free.

"Ta hell with ya then. Ta hell with the whole bunch!" Willie shouted in disgust. He tossed the remnants of his tackle into the trees and started back to the farmhouse, stomping along empty-handed, the legs and seat of his pants soaked and chafing his skin, the weight of his wet jeans dragging him down.

At the Superstore

When I drove my pickup into the parking lot, I saw a Nova Scotia licence plate on a Volvo station wagon. The car was meticulously polished and sat in the shade of the Superstore. Checking licence plates was something I had done unconsciously for a long time, and always with an eye for the Nova Scotia car. There was only one person I knew who would have been coming to Blackville from there. Had Frank Gallant come home with his wife and daughter to visit his folks as he did every summer? Frank was fussy about a car. In school when he had driven his father's, he had kept it spotless. And he was always adamant about some cause. When I glanced at the logo on this car's back bumper, "Save the something-or-other," I knew it had to be Frank's.

I looked into my rear-view mirror and adjusted the band in my hair. Then I took off my glasses, got out and slammed the truck door. I stood for a moment to look at my reflection in the window glass. I appeared shorter, my features overblown. I must get back into walking, I thought, spend less time at the computer. Then I glanced at my lopsided old truck with a lawn mower and a jug of gas in the back. Why would this have to happen to me right now, in the middle of mowing the camp grass?

I had not seen Frank Gallant since the fall of sixty-five. Really, I had moved my life back from Toronto each summer since then in hope that this would happen someday. I had always come home for my holidays. Now at the thought of seeing him, I was short of breath. I paused to try to put the whole thing into perspective. This man had played on my mind ever since we parted. Some days thoughts of him were as fleeting as a bird's shadow, at other times strong and powerful, nourished by the irreversible myth that posterity brings to a memory. Was it because of my obsessive remembering? Or had I refused to let him fade because of the way our relationship had brought me down, and I secretly wanted to prove him wrong one day? Shortly after we had split up, Frank left for Halifax to attend Dalhousie University, where he became a professor. He had married a woman from Prince Edward Island.

As I walked toward the door of the Superstore, a little breeze caught the sand in front of me and spun pebbles into my face. What if it wasn't him? I had been excited about a licence plate many times, or spotted someone in a mall, dressed in the way that Frank Gallant used to dress—shorts, sandals, and a sports jacket over a golf shirt— only to lead nowhere. Still, I knew I had to check this out. It was our hometown after all, and it was summertime, which added to the drama. It had become a secret game I played, looking for his car in parking lots and getting excited from the anticipation of meeting him, casually, so many years later. Then checking out whoever it was, and the inevitable letdown. Still, it wasn't a game that I could stop until I saw him again.

Now, when I thought of how I had always hidden things like this, the very idea that I would have kept his memory alive for thirty-odd years made me think that I should be questioning my own sanity. As recently as the week before I had dreamed of kissing Frank. I had stolen into his bedroom in some strange town and carefully kissed him on the lips without waking him. The pleasure from that dream had stayed with me for a whole day. This dream recurred through the years; in my dream, Frank looked as youthful as when I had last seen him. I knew that in reality he would not be youthful, even though it didn't seem like so many years ago. Perhaps because of the circumstances of our parting, I felt I had suffered a lot longer.

Frank Gallant had been my first love. But I had not been his first. He had told me that. I had felt inferior to Frank, felt overpowered so that I didn't know if the things I said were my own words or his. I believed he was my only real hope of finding success and happiness. After the relationship ended, I had vowed never to let anyone control my confidence. The way that he ended it all just didn't seem fair. *Once in awhile,* he had said without any warning. *It can only be once in a while from here on Sue! My parents don't want me seeing so much of you and there's my education. I'll be going away soon, and...and...and...* His words had stayed with me.

Frank had broken it off on a night shortly after we had made love for the first time. It could have been yesterday. We had been parked not far from the Superstore, behind the Boy Scout Hall in Underwood's Field. At first I had laughed, not believing him, but then I started to cry. I jumped out of the car and ran. Frank ran after me. *It's not my fault! It's not all my fault,* he kept saying. He had caught up with me and wrestled me to the ground. He tried to talk to me, even kiss me, between my boxing hands. And there in the grass I had let him, hoping that I could swing it all around to be as it had been only moments before. And I almost did.

Frank had been very upset because I cried. He apologized, saying he would take my side over his parents and we should forget the whole incident. When we went back to the car, I tried to smile, but it was shallow above the hurt. I told him I was okay. But it was never really okay after that. I always knew that it was his fault; he was only looking for someone else to blame. I had sensed even then that our relationship was never really strong from his side, and that I had been trying harder to make it work. I might have been pregnant but hadn't mentioned that to Frank. And that was how I should have left it.

When I went home later that night, I was so angry that I told my brother Gill, in confidence, that I was pregnant—that it was Frank's baby and he had just jilted me. I don't know why I did that, because deep inside I felt that our relationship was still worth nourishing. In his own right, my brother would look out for me. When Gill was drinking, well we just never knew, and I wanted to get even with Frank.

On Saturday night, outside of Ross' Canteen on Main Street, Gill hauled Frank out of his car and punched him in the face. Jill McLaren had seen everything. He broke Frank's tooth and made his nose bleed, and all the time Gill was shouting, for all to hear, *You dumped my sister mister big shot, knocked her up and dumped her!* It seemed Gill had gone a little strange that night because he kicked Frank. Jill had wiped Frank's face with a Kleenex. These were the parts that I had tried to forget. Sue Smythe pregnant and jilted by Frank Gallant had been all the talk. Jilted, yes. The fight had only served to degrade me and my family and strengthen the general sympathy for Frank. Otherwise, the breakup would have gone unnoticed.

I quit school after that, quit the fall I was going into grade eleven. I didn't go out on dates until I moved to Toronto in 1967. Through the first few years after I had dropped out of school, I hated Frank Gallant with a passion closer to love, the way that hate grows from love to become an obsession. I was never really able to reach this troubled anger to heal it. What hurt most was knowing down deep that my love for Frank was always there and that I wanted him, even then, like someone who copes with winter's bareness by grasping desperately to the spirit of spring, awaiting its return.

You see, I have never been able to find the kind of magic with another man the way I had with Frank. Everything we did together was filled with premonitions of wonderful days that lay just ahead. It was a consciousness I have never been able to recapture. Or maybe I wouldn't allow myself to find it with anyone else and clung to my memories of Frank with the hope that we might, through some ill-fated wind, unite someday. I knew that the local people who sat around their kitchen tables drinking tea and smoking, had often said, *Sue Smythe, it's a funny thing that woman never got married.*

She never seemed to bother herself about a man. And what did she do with her baby? I wonder if she's that way? Well ya never know these days do you.

Of course they did not realize that there had been relationships in Toronto. I had made several attempts, in vain perhaps. Neither did they know about all the night courses I had taken to get my degree in art theory, or the working summers in Europe as a tour guide to support myself and attempt to grow. It had all been a valuable experience, an asset when it came to writing my novels. Would Frank have read them? Probably not. Would he even be impressed with what I had done with my life? That even now, as I was entering the Superstore, my computer was receiving messages about my morning's work, which my publisher in Toronto was reading.

Maybe my books could be attributed in some ways to Frank, especially the love scenes. It was true the breakup had set a pattern for the rest of my life. Frank had inspired me to try harder. Maybe I had done all this just to impress him and was being driven by him even now. Or could it be because I was a high school dropout and always felt inferior? In any case, I had developed an overpowering hunger to succeed, if for no other reason than to prove the Gallants wrong. Frank had always been on his way to university. The Gallants were high and mighty that way. Everyone else was stupid in their eyes, especially those of us who lived out of town.

But I didn't care about any of that now, and I looked back at the whole experience as any adult looks back at their troubled teens. It was just typical small town. I had met Frank on a Saturday night in April. He stopped to give me a ride. Once I was in the car, he refused to stop driving. I can remember pretending I had other plans and wanting to get out and how proud I was, driving around the village with Frank Gallant in his father's new car. In retrospect I can see that we were never like-minded. Frank had wanted to be a professional golfer. All he had talked about was the Provincial Amateurs. I had taken an interest in golf because of him. As I looked back, it had been a summer of trying to measure up. I have often wondered how my life might have gone had I never met Frank at all.

Will he still remember me? Yes, of course he'll know me. After all, he would surely remember that he was my first love. I took a shopping cart and started to walk, glancing at things on shelves but mostly looking at men who could be him. I huddled in an aisle and adjusted myself, looking at my wrinkled jeans and my grass-stained sneakers in the reflection of a showcase.

At the produce counter a man was squinting, trying to read a label. He was tall enough and very slim, but balding behind wire-rimmed glasses. He was wearing a golf shirt, Bermuda shorts, and sandals like Frank did. But I knew I would have to see the hawklike nose. I worked my way toward him.

Yes! It was Frank Gallant not three metres away. Suddenly I could feel myself blushing, hear my own pulse as I realized I was so near him, as if he would have known that I had been in pursuit of him all this time. For an instant, I thought I might just slip away unnoticed, leave his image untarnished, young and impenetrable. Was it not better to keep it that way? It had been worth something to me through the years, inspiration if nothing else. Then I glimpsed an image of a young Frank kissing me while I caressed his tall, slim frame, feeling his weight above me that was filling my insides with a warmth I had not felt since we laid on the seat of his father's car. This was quickly followed by the memory of all the lonely nights and dull days of searching and hoping. I could not be sure which image was real, which was part of the dream. But I knew that I had to approach him now or forever live with the torment of not knowing what kind of person he had become, or what his reaction would be to meeting me so long afterwards.

Frank was talking to a sales clerk. "It's hard to find quality produce in a little village this size." It was certainly his voice, still sharp and clear. And with a cause.

"I'm sorry sir," the woman said. "The fresh produce should arrive later today." She added in a more satiric tone, "You'll have to excuse our country ways, sir."

I walked past him, close, hoping he might recognize me. I stood beside him in the aisle and adjusted the sleeve of my blouse, pretending to look at something just beyond him. He didn't notice. I turned.

"Hello Frank," I uttered as I tugged his sleeve.

At first he made no answer but looked like he was considering me through half-shut eyes. Then he spoke with a sharp and almost contemptuous tone.

"Hello." He smiled briefly, the way people do when they speak to older people they don't even know. He had the same broken tooth.

"Frank, it's me! Sue Smythe. Remember?" I heard myself say this just as I had so often in my dreams.

"Sue!" He turned and hugged me.

"I saw you standing here and I thought, 'Now that man looks familiar,' and then…" My hands were playing with the gold chain around my neck.

"Oh yes, Sue. Of course I remember you. We used to…" He stepped back, but before he could say anything more I came forward and hugged him again. During this hug he kissed me on the cheek.

"Hey, it's great to see you again," I said.

"Sue Smythe. Well now, it's like old times, the two of us together. And you're just as pretty as you ever were." He was clinging to my elbow as he talked.

"So-o-o, are you just home for holidays?" I was having trouble keeping my voice even. I took a deep breath. It was the old days again, but the old days toward the end. For an instant I was sorry I had approached him, and I wanted to withdraw.

"Yes. I'm home. Mom's not all that well and. . ." Frank's forehead furrowed and he held his stare, one hand playing with his shirt collar.

"I live here in the summer now, eh. I've built a river camp on the old property up home. I might stay here full-time someday. I love the river, you know." I immediately wondered if I should have said this.

"Yes someone told me you did. But can you live comfortably in an old cabin on the river that way? I could see it for maybe for a few weeks in the summer, but…well, whatever."

"Oh yes, it's wonderful out there. The river is beautiful."

"And did I hear somewhere that you are writing now?"

"Just a little." It was obvious he hadn't read my work.

"Well good for you, Sue! Anyway, I'm here for only a week. My daughter is coming from Charlottetown in a few days. She's down there visiting her grandparents. We'll drive back together."

"I always thought you might move home someday. You and you're wife." As I said this I immediately wished I could have retracted it.

Frank's face reddened. "My wife and I are parted. She divorced me right after my operation. You know, I had a triple bypass three years ago. I'm still living with my daughter, Susan, in my own house on University Avenue in Halifax. It's a good end of town. There's a doctor next door, a lawyer down the street."

"So you've done okay then," I said, thinking, Is this really Frank Gallant? "I mean, you're happy?" I was twirling my glasses.

"Well, let me put it this way, I try to keep busy. Susan's good company and a woman comes in twice a week to do the cleaning. She's even more meticulous than I am, if you can believe that. She keeps the house spotless. No, I think I would go crazy if I had to live alone. But yes, I thought about moving home, for awhile after the divorce. I guess it took me some time to get domesticated. Believe me, I thought about doing that very thing. And then I thought but what if something happens to Mother, look where I'd be. I learned she had willed the old house to my sister. That didn't go down too well, as you can imagine, after all I did for her. There's not much to do around here anyway. And Mom doesn't even have cable TV. Can you imagine! I'm going up the frigging walls here."

"It depends on what you're looking for, I guess."

"Well, the old village seems sort of dull. And the old crowd is all gone. I don't know the younger ones. But one time, my God, I thought the centre of the universe was right here in Blackville."

"My God, yes. And remember Geo's canteen?" I was instantly sorry this slipped out and I tried to cover. "Remember the time we went to Oak Point?"

Frank reddened again. "Yes, I suppose I do. Was that after a movie or something? No, I guess that was another time with…"

"No, no. We went to Oak Point on a Sunday afternoon, you and I. Your father's car broke down and we had to hitchhike home. Remember?"

"Imagine." Frank said distractedly. It was clear he didn't.

"We have a golf course now. Do you still play?" I ventured.

"I play a bit, but mostly I watch it on TV. Honest Sue, I think that is why I keep on teaching. I can't see myself retiring until they push me out. I think I would go crazy if I had to be idle."

I had often thought about writing Frank to tell him that my pregnancy was all a lie, but he had never inquired about it and was avoiding the subject now.

"So-o-o, you're still single then?" he said as he looked over his glasses into the produce bin.

"Yes, I guess I am." I could not help chuckling. I thought, This is the man who has been living inside me for all these years? Where was my head in the sixties?

"And living way out there alone, in a river camp as you call it?"

"That's me!"

"Look, maybe before I go back, I'll see what I have left for time, but I guess I could call you. We could get together, maybe do lunch or something. I guess we have a lot of catching up to do. Who knows. I have a feeling you would like that." He spoke without turning around.

"Oh, I don't know, I…"

Frank turned again and reached out to touch my hand. "How about it Sue? Whatta ya say? Why don't we do it?" He flashed the same smile from before, the smile I had once thought…well, I don't know, now, what I had been thinking. "Do you have a telephone out there at the river?"

"No, actually I don't. You won't be able to reach me that way, " I said. "Are you on-line?"

"No! God no, not yet. I've been putting it off. I guess I have to get into it, as everyone is nowadays."

"Look, why don't I call you…" I was gesturing with my hands, hoping he would not pursue it. Then I turned away quickly and put on my glasses so I could read the ingredients on a box of pasta.

Autumn

September Morning

It has been a cool night. I should have closed the front door. My sleep is disturbed by the sharp staccato whistle of the osprey. I turn in my bed, experiencing the mingling and melting away of night dreams. Half-conscious, I can hear a pulp truck on the distant chip-seal road. That would be my friend Donny Brophy going to work. He is a trucker who lives just up the highway in what used to be my uncle's farmhouse. There is a grey dawn at the window, a late summer chill.

You lie beside me with your face to the wall. I put an arm about your waist and pull you to me, knowing that tonight I will be alone in this bed, scenting your perfume on the pillow, reliving this summer of loving you. And trying to justify letting you go without a struggle. Tomorrow, I think, learning how to live alone begins again. But now there is a calm and I lay and wait for the osprey's territorial signal but hear only the hollow gurgle of the brook nearby and the buzz of a housefly in the lighted bathroom.

I get up and stagger to the bath, have a drink of water, then I go to the screened door to look at the river. Subtle, ever so subtle waves move out across the water from the brook's mouth where the salmon are lying in the colder water. The river itself is warm, low and clear. I can smell its bottom along the shores where the water has dropped: decaying algae, sun-baked stones, clam shells, life jackets, and sweaty sneakers. There are junks of foam adrift in the channel. They crowd together in the run like lemmings. Later they will make moving shadows against the amber bottom before burning off as the sun strengthens.

Higher along the opposite shore is the dewed meadow grass, tall and silent, now showing a few strands of yellow. The grassy hillside beyond is yellow with wildflowers. The trees, double green, are now tinted slightly. And beyond the trees, the lofty pink sky. Everything is tranquil, even holy, the way that Sunday's drive home from church used to be from the back seat of my father's car when I was a child. In my mind, I try two cadenzas in the scene. First Pachelbel's Canon in D, then J. S. Bach's Gavotte in D Major. These do not do justice to the morning, and I block them out. Then the little brook rises up to sing, chuckle, gurgle, gulp. This is the better score, I think.

I stand behind the screen door in my shorts and T-shirt. No breeze yet, not a whisper. The grass in the yard is silver with dew. The boardwalk to the woodshed is silver, as is my car windshield. And now a raven whoops, some kind of warning I suspect. Or maybe it is trying to out-sing the brook (as I did a few moments ago). A red squirrel runs from limb to limb in the trees that hug our cabin. It stops to scold at my presence in the doorway. And I realize, only now, that I do not have the senses keen enough to see and feel the whole picture in the way of the raven and the squirrel. But of course I love it just as much. This place is all I know, because, you see, I have never been away. Not even for the winter like the osprey or the crane. And because this is my whole life, I now take some comfort in the fact that this is not a rainy day. Rain, I think, would bring down a power failure right now.

I look into the bedroom where you are sleeping. Only your face is exposed above the covers. Your long lashes are pretty upon faded summer cheeks. Pretty lashes that hide dark passionate eyes, full of thought, full of love, revealing your feelings long before you say a thing. You think these parts of you are nothing, but I know them to be the nothingness of greatness. In your eyes, too, are the lingering images of a daddy's little girl, freckled and skinny with twisted sandals, denim jeans, ball cap, and the sunglasses you found in the river. You have been your mother's loyal daughter, too, postured with earrings, pantyhose, a touch of makeup, but always keeping that awkward smile that is real and the youthful spirit. Even with me you have been crazy and funny, mature and graceful, tomboyish, a fishing partner for years, and a true lover with eyes that drew me to them with a moisture so rich and deep that whoever you looked at fell in love with you. I think of our years together. You and I on the river, skating, sailing, fishing, and this old cabin. I wish I could do it all again, but only with you.

Now, all of the years are suddenly condensed into two small images. Our old boat is under sail and you are standing at the back with both hands on the rudder bar, your slim bathing-suited body braced against the rail, hair stringy, shrill voice singing (after just one beer) a sea shanty you hardly even know. You are trying to impress me. This is followed by a comfort in the way you embrace me when I am down. These images come together now, embracing and singing, embracing and singing. They dance like ghosts in a mourning fog.

You will be leaving today, to go to the University of Toronto. This is your chance to grow, get sophisticated. When you come back, you will be a different Carol. You will have set aside your local river dialect, your corny humour, your homely innocent warmth, that summer spirit. In a sense you will never return. Not really. Not the way you are. Changes, new ideas will have made you ashamed of who you are and where you come from. Ideas will govern your spirit and refine your posture so that you will stay always and irreversibly within their boundaries, not yours. And not mine.

Later this morning I will kiss you goodbye and try not to show emotion as you drive away. I realize now that I cannot help you through tomorrow. I have no more nourishment, no new philosophic direction in which to lead you. You might say that I have been your

April man, a spectator who has watched you grow beyond me, watched you pine and suffer within yourself because you did so. Though you have always loved me for the man that I am. Now, the most important thing to me is that you keep growing to make this hurt worth something. I could ask you to stay for my own selfish reasons because I know you love me enough to do it. Maybe you do. But I can not stand still and watch you become me. Not for a minute. You would. I guarantee it.

So I sit at my computer to write this secret note to you while you are still sleeping and before the day gets hot. I will put this in your suitcase, there in the back pocket where your writing paper and family photos are. You will read it in your room in Toronto someday down the road and think of me with that goodness of yours. I hope. Somewhere on the river, in the same instant, I will think of you. And I will remember you just the way you are this morning.

A Fall Ailment

The fall when I was eight years old and in grade two was a time in my life that my brother Jack, my little sister Sonya and I had to stop and wonder just who our real parents were. Our big house was full of family and relations, as old homesteads sometimes are. Grandparents lived in, and aunts and uncles came and went, sometimes staying a week or a month. Always one of us (or them) was laid up, especially in the fall of the year. The Hong Kong and the Asian flu were names given to household illnesses, and the measles, mumps, and chicken pox were suffered in sequence as a matter of course. There was the dreaded pleurisy, pneumonia, and infantile paralyses, which we all feared but were lucky enough never to have contracted. My mother never got sick and took care of us all. So when *she* became ill on Halloween 1952, we hardly took notice and hoped it would not prevent her from helping us with our costumes and making fudge for a party that night at Nick's father's barn.

My mother, Dorothy Mckann, who was really a northwest Henry, moved to The Forks to live with her mother after her father died, which was where my father met her at a party. She had been a chambermaid since the age of twelve, working in our community before marrying my father and moving into this place at age seventeen. She was like all the northwest Henrys, strong and tireless, a clean housekeeper, and a good cook. She also helped our father in his small country store. She worked so hard at times that even we children could sense she suffered the delusion that her work ethic was the reason she was brought here. But of course this was not true. My father loved her and often told her so. Because my family were river people and had employed Henry women before, my mother felt inferior. *A nor'west Henry, a good work-horse of a maid,* she called herself when she felt taken advantage of, but she worked harder, her wild red hair symbolic of an internal rage and her struggle to keep a civil tongue.

So it was hard for any of us children to imagine our mother sick in bed with Gram and Aunt Edith waiting on her—a strange and not-so-funny Halloween joke. The illness had come instantly, an inexplicable turn of events. In the morning she had made breakfast for everyone and sent us out to play, like any Saturday. Later she helped Father with the storm windows, washing them and passing them up the ladder to him. It was then she took a pain and went into the house to lay down. When we came in from the river for lunch, mother was in bed, and already the doctor had been called.

It was the coldest and greyest autumn that I can remember. The big rains had come early and soaked the fields so that the frost and the winds bleached them a pale orange, and the corrugated ploughed land melted into faded chocolate and froze, as potatoes and turnips were hurried into cellar bins, layered in cakes of mud. Along the road on our way to school, matted leaves stuck to our rubber boots like slippery wet newspapers, and by Halloween it had already snowed, forcing us to wear winter coats and mittens.

Early in the fall my father had bought a good second-hand shearling coat from a widower in the village whose wife had died during childbirth the spring before. My mother wore it to church on Sundays. I was superstitious about the coat, and whenever she put it on I thought of the dead woman in the village and the two daughters my age she had left behind. But what I remember most about that particular fall was the dampness. It seemed to go right through a coat or a scarf. And my mother's illness.

In the early afternoon Doctor Boudreau came to the house. He was a young doctor who had moved recently to the river. He seemed indecisive and unsure of himself. Sensing this, we had no confidence in him whatsoever.

"He sends everyone to the hospital," I heard Mr. Vickers say to Aunt Edith in my father's store.

When Sonya and I went into Mother's room that afternoon, she was lying in bed staring dry-eyed at the ceiling, with a bunch of Kleenex in her grip. Her hair was wild as a bale of carrots. The doctor had hoisted her iron rung bed, stacking books under the legs so that Mother's feet were higher then her head.

When I asked mother what was wrong, she said softly, "Nothing Bobby. Now you just go out and play with the others. I'll be all right!"

Gram took me by the elbow and told me I must go downstairs and be quiet. Sonya, who was six, protested, but once Mother assured her that everything was okay, we went out to play. It seemed that only a catastrophe could spoil a Saturday, especially if it was Halloween. Still, as we ran in the fields and down by the river that afternoon, playing hide-and-seek or cowboys and Indians, every once in a while I would be struck by an image of Mom propped up in her bed. The others would catch me staring and shake me from my reverie.

Every so often we ran inside and up to her room to see how she was, only to be ushered away by Gram or Aunt Edith. Downstairs, Father had come in from his work and sat in a rocker in the hall, staring at the wallpaper. Later, I listened at the door to overhear him telling Gram that it was all a terrible mis-something-or-other, this illness that mother had somehow brought on herself. I wondered what had she done.

Everyone in our community smoked then and our store shelves along one wall were lined with pretty red, blue, and yellow packages of cigarettes with the photos of sailors and pretty women and frightened black Halloween cats: Players, Vogue, ZigZag, and Black Cat. We had stolen a pack of Black Cats. Nick kept Father looking for a cardboard box at the back while Jack reached over the counter for the pack of tailor-mades. Later, at our camp on the riverbank, we smoked as Jack, the oldest, reasoned that there could be a new baby come out of our mother's sickness and it had something to do with Mom and Dad sleeping together. Our family seemed the perfect size the way it was. As we talked about this, one of us got dizzy and another got sick, but we all got hooked on tobacco that day.

"Is Mom going to have a baby?" I was out of breath, having run to the house to ask Dad.

"Not likely!" he snapped. "Now you just go outside and play with the others, and don't bother us." He pushed me out of his line of view from where he had been staring at the wall.

"But Jack said she is sick and she is going to have a baby!" And then I said the "no" words. "From sleeping with you!"

"Now you just hold your tongue about such things and go play!". Sonya said, "Daddy could I have a new baby sister?" she grinned. "Outside!"

"The doctor brings a baby in his suitcase if there's any to be brought." Aunt Edith put in.

At this I started to pound on my father's legs. "But I don't want to go outside! I want to be with my Mommy. What did you do to Mommy? I hate you!" I cried.

Sonya chimed in, "I want to be with my Mommy! I hate you!"

Gram whisked us off to the dining room. She convinced us that everything would be okay. I worried that Father must have hated Sonya and I then.

In the early evening Nick came with the news that his father would not let us use the barn for the Halloween party because he was afraid of fires. Instead he was going to hold the party at a grove in a gully where we used to play. By evening it was cold, and it had started to rain. The doctor came back to our house and everyone was looking quite grim, so the Halloween party was cancelled. Gram kept Jack and Sonya and I in the dining room, standing with us in a circle like a mother hen with chicks and she prayed and sang hymns the way she used to do during a lightning storm. We all knew, by then, that there was something terribly wrong with our mother.

What we did not know until later that night was that while we were confined to the dining room, the ambulance (really an old hearse) had backed up to our front door, and the driver (really the undertaker from Blackville) and Dad had carried Mom down the stairs on a stretcher and put her in the back. When we came out of the dining room, we could sense that something had happened. Jack and I ran upstairs. Mother's room was dark and empty. Only then Gram told us that they had taken her to the hospital in Newcastle, which to me, then, was a place where they took people to die.

We were put to bed after Gram made us kneel on the floor in the upstairs hall to say our prayers. We prayed mostly for Mom before repeating the Lord's Prayer after Gram. Jack and I and Sonya climbed into the big double bed together. When Gram had gone downstairs and everything was quiet, we got out of bed and tiptoed to our mother's room again. Her bed was not made and the room was an unusual shambles along with lingering smells of ointments, blue soaps, and the full chamber pots under the tilted bed. We returned to our own room and, under the covers, whispered about what we thought might have been happening.

"What would it be like to have Gram for a mother?" I asked.

Jack said, "Shut up Bobby, just you shut up right now."

Sonya started to cry, but only for a minute before Gram shouted for us to be quiet. Jack, who was two years older than me, seemed to understand mother's sickness, but he did not know how it came about. Father's mood that day made it easy for us to blame him. We united in a conspiracy of hate. When neighbours dropped by out of curiosity, we listened to them talking downstairs and tried to understand what was happening to our lives.

"She's not expected to live the night!" We heard Gram say to Mr. Vickers when he came in. "The poor soul, she's awful low surely." A sense of panic fell over us. Sonya started to cry again.

She kept asking, "Is it morning yet. What time is it Bobby? Is she still away? Is she still alive?" Sonya cried until Gram came up to our room to tell us stories. My sister dropped off to sleep. I slept a little but not deeply enough to let go of the trauma. It seemed like every time I closed my eyes, I would see that shearling coat, worn first by a dead woman in the village and then by my mother. I eased out of bed to sneak a look in the closet in my mother's room. The coat was not there; she must have taken it with her.

No one came trick or treating at our house that night. Not one soul. At times we rose from our bed to look out the window, trying to catch a glimpse of a signalling firecracker that might arc in the darkness along the highway and distract us from the drama. It wasn't even like Halloween, rather a hush and chilly fall night. Across the river at the Vickers' farm, someone was burning potato stocks in spite of the rain and the brown smoke that drifted over the fields was sweet like the scent of a rum-dipped cigar. The only sound was a dog that barked in the distance and then answered its own echo.

For a brief period the following morning, we awoke to a normal household before the memories of the previous night surfaced. There had been no word from the hospital, but we had overheard Gram say to Aunt Edith in the kitchen that our mother had lost a baby. Where, we wondered, had she lost it? Jack said that it was something called a miscarriage, which Father refused to talk to us about. Had it been our fault? We hung around the house and lived through the news of my mother's death every time the telephone rang. Later when Gram phoned the hospital, word was sent that she was the same, then later in the day stable, and finally some better. At this news we were bundled up and sent outside to play in the clearing November Sunday.

In the afternoon Father sat in the rocker by the stove and told Mr. Vickers how he had fainted when he tried to call the ambulance. "I just got dizzy and passed out at the sound of the undertaker's voice on the line," he said. "Edith here had to take the receiver." We listened as he told Mr. Vickers that the sound of the ambulance siren was still in his ears. On their way to the hospital, he said that in Bridgetown there was an old house on the road and the driver had to go through a field to get around it. Once he had to get out of the car to clear away road blocks and was hit on the chest with a big rotten egg. When our father mentioned being hit by the egg, he smiled faintly and shook his head. Then we all laughed as hard as we could.

It seemed that fall there were always clouds the colour of rats hanging over the river, drifting in winds that turned the grey water choppy. The slanting rains became more chilling with the days and my father's black-and-white cows squelched in crooked trails of mud through the swamp pasture to stand by the bars and bawl to be let into the barn. We set our clocks back. Darkness obscured our vision and the dampness made little rainbows at the edges of our flashlight beams as we stacked soggy firewood into the sheds or raked matted leaves from the dooryard long after crayoned jack-o-lanterns and black bats had been taken from windows and our burnt-out pumpkin, pelted by slingshot stones, had fallen to the ground and broken into tiny new moons. We craved the fudge that mother wasn't able to make us and our cotton sack costumes lay in a heap on the floor of the cold summer kitchen.

Aunt Edith told us that, whatever we did, we were not to miss school because mother was away and sick. She would want us to be good scholars while she was gone. Because Edith had once been a teacher (though not well herself now) she helped us with our homework. In the schoolhouse Mrs. Jardine, in her mundane voice, went over the spelling of foreign lands and drew maps on the blackboards. Sonya and I tried desperately to concentrate but couldn't. Our teacher didn't ask us any questions through the days that mother was ill. She seemed to understand we were distracted by home problems. And I was grateful. In the schoolyard during recess, the bigger children also seemed to favour us in the games we played. It was from these boys and girls that we learned more about mother's illness.

In the evenings the old men of the community, Mr. Vickers and others, came to the store, walking through the woods carrying deer rifles which they stood in the corner while they smoked and joked with my father, who seemed indifferent to them now as well as to us children. He was so preoccupied with Mom's illness.

One of them would ask, "How's the wife, Eldon?"

He would reply, "Oh the same I guess, well some better last I heard." Then he would change the subject to deer hunting.

At home, we tried to fit Gram into our mother's shoes. We knew that living without mom would take plenty of getting used to and it was just as well to get started right away because we didn't expect her back at this point, not really. We quit asking questions. We did not know what to believe because no neighbours had come by in days, so there was no opportunity to hide behind a door and listen while a family member explained Mom's condition. The whole episode seemed to be drawn out of some incomprehensible dream inspired by that dead woman's coat, which carried the ghost of motherless children. I thought it would have been better for the family in the village to at least keep that part of their mother, to hang on to the coat.

Then the snow came. It sifted through the bare trees like rice, bending down grass to leave bare pockets under little crystal caves with embroidered edges that glowed red in the sunset. There was a kind of excitement in this. The snow thawed and froze again and crunched under our rubbers like rotting wood shingles. Mom had been gone for about three weeks, and we were starting to get used to having Gram and Aunt Edith for our mother. It was rough, but it was working in a way.

One day after school, as I was carrying the night's firewood into the house, I overheard Gram telling Aunt Edith that Mother would be coming home that evening. It seemed as though someone was about to return from the dead, someone we had been praying to return but not really expecting it, the way that prayers go. We had suffered her being taken from us the way she was, and had grown used to living without her. Her coming home made all that suffering seem for nothing. Gram and Aunt Edith together had become our surrogate mothers. Still, I ran out into the shed, kneeled in the sawdust, and closed my eyes.

"Thank you God," I said. "Thank you for answering my prayers this one time."

Later, when I saw the car coming into the driveway, I ran as fast as I could from the river to the house. Our farm had suddenly filled with an afternoon blast of light. Mother was a pretty woman in her thirties then. Dressed in her green velvet suit and the shearling coat, her pallor was like skim milk. She sat in the hall rocker with everyone crowded around her. I went to the doorway and stood petulant, looking into the room.

She was telling everyone, "It's so great to be home. I didn't expect to get back alive!" Then she laughed a little, like she wanted to share it all with us, and we craved to hear everything. When she saw me, she said, "And there's my little darling Bobby with the big sad eyes!" She put out her hands as if to pull me near her. But I could not move. Instead I blushed and squirmed and held my position in the doorway, though I wanted so badly to go to her and experience that familiar warmth, the scent of her breath. "Come and give me a big hug now, Bobby!" she canted her head shyly and smiled. "Please?" I could not force myself to do this because there were so many in the room. "My soul, Bobby, you need a haircut. And that old shirt you have on, my God look at you!" Then she turned to Gram. "The children didn't have much of a Halloween this year." For a moment I resented the timing of her illness, and I wanted to suggest that we dress up funny and have our fudge that night.

My mother sat rocking as she told the family that in the hospital she had received transfusions because she had lost a lot of blood and was very weak, but that she could feel her strength coming back slowly. Every time she closed her eyes she saw Bobby's sad eyes the way he had looked upstairs on the day she left. "Now, Bobby would you come here and give me a hug. Please?" I stood my ground. She said that in the hospital she could see only the cold metal room with the intravenous machine and drip lines with their moving bubbles. So she would close her eyes again and then it was little Sonya's sweet face and her tousled red hair. These images inspired her to get better, she said, more than anything the doctors had done.

Mother hoped we hadn't missed much school, and she spoke about what a shame it was that we couldn't visit her for the whole three weeks because children were not allowed in hospitals.

"That's just the way it is in the city, so foolish, " she said. Then she told us that a woman had died in the room beside her. "Such a nice person, too, with the same illness I had." She reached into her purse for a handkerchief to wipe her eyes.

Sonya said, "But what did she die from Mommy, the other woman?"

"Oh just some kind of fall ailment, I don't think the doctor knew himself. " She winked at Gram and Aunt Edith and started to spell e-x-p-e-c-t-i-n-g and, later in the conversation, p-r-e-g-n-a-n-t, which made me blush. I hoped she would stop spelling because I now knew what these words meant.

I could not come forward to hug my mother and stood peevishly in the doorway. Sonya hugged her legs and tugged on her hands then ran bobbing up and down the hall in her little white dress she had put on for the occasion. Her red hair flared out like Mom's and she flashed her awkward toothless grin as she bowed and spun around and around to make her dress fan out in a balloon in front of Mother, who sat in the rocker laughing. Then Sonya put her hands on Mother's knee. "Did you bring us something from the hospital? Could we open up the suitcase now, please?"

There Are Two Rivers Here

We are into October, towards Thanksgiving. The wind is picking up and the nights are cold, freezing cold already. It seems the weather has changed overnight. All summer here, in the early mornings, I've been sitting down to work on a novel. When you're busy like that, time just slips away. Already I regret not having done enough canoeing, fishing, or hosting old friends and family for barbecues. But next year, before the weather turns. Next year.

The wind is darker now, and there are spits of rain, maybe a hailstone here and there to lodge and not melt on some decayed leaf, or on the pathway to the woodshed. There is sighing in the pine trees, rattling and moaning in the eavestroughs. Ghosts. Here on the river, there are always ghosts in the wind, voices in the trees. I think now of the ghosts of winter, of great-grandparents and grandparents long dead. I think, too, of the ghosts of summer and parents and potluck meals, ghosts of spring and my unsure young self, of old loves long gone, of my own family and friends. I don't see much of them anymore. These ghosts skitter between yesterday and tomorrow. There are even ghosts of fading dreams, ghosts of other ghosts, you might say. Voices in the wind make them bright now and full of spirit, like youthful spring days, these images embroidered by the magic of time. You see, it's a question of magic.

In a day or two I will close up camp and move to the city for another winter. In a day or two…I've been putting it off.

I have been here since April.

I have been here for five generations.

The Miramichi is where my great-great grandparents immigrated from England in 1818 and where many of my family (including myself in summer) still live. She flows from the centre of New Brunswick, northeast to the sea—one hundred and fifty miles of washed gravel, twisting through backyards, fields and woods, audible from dooryards, always within reach, always within view. Our houses are little white boxes like sugar cubes on hillsides that overlook the river. *We see the river differently,* my father would say. *There are really two rivers here, you know, ours and theirs.*

Statistically, it is said to be one of the best salmon streams anywhere, truly a great place to fish. But we are not much into statistics. We are practical minded, long on sensitivity, impulsiveness, and experience. We are the sons and daughters of the river. To the sport fishers who write for outdoor magazines, this river is one of boots and borons, Polaroids and patterns, ponchos and parkas; of tippets, tailers, tilles, and tweeds; vests and visors, canes and cameras—and forty-five-pounders.

Ours is more a river of old relations, old bones, old dreams gone sour and new dreams nurtured and made real. Ours is a river made of blood streams. Yes, through the years we have killed our share of fish. But this is not something we take pride in. As part of growing up, we have learned to provoke the impulsive salmon to take a fly hook. We have become at one with the fish's state of mind, the river's condition the way one family member might sense what another is thinking after a while. This is not done for pleasure, exactly, nor spoken about much. Because we do it for different reasons, our catches are never literally weighed or measured.

When I look through old albums, I see photos of family members, standing with two or three sport fishers (whose names are long since forgotten) with a dozen salmon spread on the grass before them. Perhaps these were from a day's fishing at the home pool here on the Miramichi, or maybe they are catches from three-day runs down the Cains—a common event after my father started outfitting in the 1950s. Also in those old albums I see myself, my brothers, and sister, children fixing a sail to a canoe, paddling a board boat, or posing on the roof of some fishing camp still under construction. When my sister got her first salmon at age seven, an American sportsman photographed her standing in the boat holding it. She was wearing a little print dress and her freckled face was beaming—the only pose of its kind in the album.

Everyone in my family owns a river camp. My cabin is on the old family homestead, on a giant loop in the river the fishermen call the Golden Horseshoe because of its excellent spring salmon catches. We called the place Camp Oriole, not after the fly hook but the bird.

My father and I built the cabin thirty years ago from logs we cut on his woodlot. It has an open veranda facing the river but no fireplace yet, just an air-tight stove. In front of the camp, on calm spring days, the motorboat-wrinkled water sparkles in the sun as guides hunch in their anchored boats, telling their seated guests where to cast. Their S-shaped lines uncoil across the water and they stare tentatively at the swinging streamers for the doughnut-shaped boil of a striking salmon. As I work in the yard I can hear their voices, smell their perfume: cigar smoke blending with gasoline.

Yesterday I fed my pet moose birds more crumbs than usual, gave my squirrels an extra helping of peanuts. I hope they will be around next spring. I have put the canoe in already, tucked lawn chairs under the veranda, and dismantled the water pipes. I have walked around the grounds many times and down to the shore where the upriver wind brings a tear. Maybe tomorrow I will leave.

In the city I will take courses, go to the theatre, art shows, movies, hockey games, and the occasional night club when I feel the need for a bright woman to talk with. And wait for spring. By mid-March I will have already started packing to return. (if I've bothered to unpack). I will be here to witness the heavy winds and the spring rains and the ice floes that come with the arrival of the new season. The rumble of ice, the hollering of crows, the smell of melting snow. I will sit and watch the reflections of my fire through the glass doors of the stove, listen to cars on the distant chip-seal highway, contemplate where in the woods each log in the wall has grown. I will scent the tar and oakum between the logs, the burnt ash of the stove and, as if I suddenly understand something, try to put my life into perspective. Again.

On April mornings, the strong northeast winds come scudding up the river to make my windows rattle and the stovepipes creak, toss pine boughs to make them whisper and turn silver in the sun. I will sit on the veranda steps and smoke, like old times. In April, before the run-off, the water is always low and ink-coloured with moving patches of black and little white crests riding the waves.

I will pick my way to the water between miniature icebergs melting to look like half-carved polar bears. There will be ice adrift and a dark blanket of clouds, but snow will be indifferent to the wind. Along the opposite shore, naked alders like pen strokes will emulate a woods black and silent beyond. I will smoke and huddle in the lee of rotting ice and tie a smelt streamer to the leader. And, as in a recurring dream, I will try to cast against the wind into the current, cast and strip so my streamer moves in spurts like a small fish in distress. I will cast as far as I can. The sour shore and budding leaf smells will be familiar, as will the voice of birds. This dream that resurfaces from past seasons is a journey inside, is this other river we call ours. And what is more truthful than a dream?

You see, the other river is the one the tourists use. These people drive the river roads in station wagons, elbows out the window, fishing rods slanting down the roofs. They are into a more transient river, more shallow, faster running, more strategic. We read their where-to-and-how-to in the outdoor magazines and raise an eyebrow. "Try the riffled hitch," they write. "Cast a tight loop—up river—and mend."

Sure, sure. Our own presentations are never just physical. Our river runs much deeper. Like most river people, my father has a mythical image of the home stream and he loves it, so that when he started outfitting in the 1950s, he said he felt like a prostitute. We are held in a bond by the river, tied by heartstrings in a marriage with an ecosystem. We are more in tune with the river and its creatures. But we share another stream in a sense, the river that is ever present inside us. While we never take the literal stream for granted and share in its protectiveness and indeed its defence, the river inside is more sacred. More than that, the moods of our river are so powerful in a sense they control our state of mind, a consciousness that comes of living with the river for generations.

We observe (almost without looking) the colours of the water brought on by the sky and how this translates into moods. I wish I could accurately describe the river dawns, the middays, and the sunsets, and what feelings they stir in us. We watch others, even tourists, whose feelings are more obvious and carry more truth at dawn, when that first tint of drab comes out of the night sky and makes the river orange, bringing with it the sounds of morning, reflecting a series of new horizons, new hope for us all. Birds sing, trees sigh and touch us with their sounds and scent, and we taste the coming day. We wonder if these things have anything to do with how we regard ourselves at this time, with an undistorted view, a self-analyzing look, and say *Oh God,* as if we were being reinstated once more to try it all again. The river has humbled us in this way. I wish I could tell you how the sun appears over the shadowy trees and climbs against a pale blue ceiling, turns the crystal water charcoal then black with the help of a subtle breeze. How this changes our feelings. And how this open sky and breeze carry us, sometimes aimlessly, to new hope, until our new-made plans of morning are trodden upon by complacency, overtaken by practicalities, only to resurface when the dawn breaks through again.

I wish I could explain how in the afternoons, when the colours of sky and water start to wane, and the sun makes ghosts of us all with its lengthening, kinked, twisted shadows, we sometimes sing our own praises in defence of who we are. We know we can't really change who we are nor can we shake the ghosts of our past, which we know all too well, as everyone else on the river knows. This is the small price we pay for living here so long. But there are times when I feel a real sense of comfort only here, with other river people.

So we defend each other and our reasons for being here; we are at home nowhere else. These feelings recur in our sons and daughters, the way they did in our grandparents and parents. It's a generational, a genealogical pattern. The sun and water carry us along, until tired and weary at day's end we commence an internal cleansing of despair and regrets. Like the river, we sometimes appear unsure of new direction. At evening we rationalize the fading away of morning dreams, our inability to make them real, and we replace them with a kind of ease; they have become frivolous.

When the sun has begun to set, and the lavenders and reds reflect the spectacular cloud formations upon the water once more, we are taken to our rest. We leave the country and river, let it close in behind us. The trees whisper evening sounds that forgive us our failed attempts to reach new goals. We are consoled by the trees, water and sky. The river is a sheet of moving steel, flowing between smoky green strips, its treetops a saw blade on the horizon. A jagged cloud points across the pink sky, turning the river pink, but silver where the water runs faster. Pink ducks fly in a wedge toward the sea, buttermilk and whipped cream form on the eddies, and a vapour trail forms behind a sunlit silver bullet beyond sound, on its way to Europe. Already there is a charcoal tint to the woods and gravel beach, and the old boat with its pole and gas can have become a silhouette. There is the hollow sound of a car on the distant highway. A chill comes over us. We savour the warmth stirred from old ashes. In a sense we are reliving past dawns, clinging to past sunsets like a child does a toy, just for the simple pleasures it brings.

A copper cloud rises, a Matterhorn-like fog to hold the reflection one minute longer. Windows blaze. We sit up and marvel at the beauty and think that if it happens again we will move with it but in a different way next time. If it all would just happen again, one more time. But we watch as the mountain turns into a blimp and drifts away. There are the desperate honks of a lost duck, smothered by the increasing sounds of water in the hollow air.

The sun drops behind trees that have darkened to black. The water has gone from pink to blue to lavender and is a now a mirror reflecting a galaxy of stars. We retreat once more and watch as it runs on into the darkness, only to repeat itself in us again at dawn. These are subtleties and nothing more, the reflections of sky upon water, the moods the river stirs in us.

It has to do with who we are, and why we are here. We have become passionate about our river, the way true lovers are passionate about one another. After a while, the seasons blend and become one long season. Trees bud then blossom into tiny rabbit paws of hope. They grow white along black stems into veined and wrinkled palms that whisper in currents of breeze. They sigh, twist, and murmur in the gales of summer and eventually fall, when our bonfires smoulder in the comforting haze of autumn. The seasons of our lives have overlapped. The same different things come to us every year, and we share them in a sense. They have nothing to do with fish or fishing and everything to do with you and me.

Much of this river has been sold to foreign investors. They have deeds in office drawers in American and Swiss banks, and they pay taxes on riparian rights, which they come to fish in summertime. So many have come and gone through the years, and there are still more to come, seeking what dollars or francs can never really buy. How do you buy a river? A piece of paper in a foreign bank does not account for much, really. Not here. Foreigners have the ownership, but we have the river. We believe that no river can ever be claimed or owned by any man or woman. It would be like trying to buy a piece of sky—a spectacular cloud formation or a forlorn sunset—or to purchase a state of mind, a family member, or a long-sought lover without winning their heart. The river stays and flows among its own, its family. We have endured and survived here together, and no one becomes part of it in a single generation, or even two. We have been taught this by the river itself.

Since 1818 the river has leaked into my family's bloodstreams like a virus and grown with us, around us, and through us, controlling, even haunting us. It has taken time. Old time, slow time. Our slow-moving river has become an ancient parent whose history flows not from ice ages or avalanches aeons ago, but from some holy sanctuary of stained glass. A mystical and storied ancestor, at times babbling and shallow, at times deep and moody, then frothing, and unforgiving. Always it has the same message, *I love you all, I love you all.* Her dominating presence demands a big part of us, perhaps because she is always receptive, possessing different healing powers.

This ol' river keeps us sane, Father used to say. *Whenever we are unsure of who we are and where we are going and are weary of life's considerations, we head for the river.* He has always spoken of the river like an old relative, in tones positive and a bit defensive. Old relatives rise to embrace and console their children. We feel this.

This is the same old river where the log drivers in their hobnailed boots cuffed the logs and sang the shanty songs that were unfit for women's ears. To the tune of fiddlers they ran from log to log, my great-grandfathers and grandfathers among them, their faces bronzed from the sun, their long poles striking the water for balance. My father for much of his life was a lumberman, a guide, and an outfitter on this river. The same river where I took my first job guiding, the fall I quit school in 1960, then a natural thing to do. For us children the river was our ball park, golf course, paper route, movie house, and hockey rink. The river was something to admire and respect, like an ageing grandparent whose images I can still see: gaspereau nets hung on pickets or over beams in sheds to dry, dugout boats, salmon spears, and bolt-hook poles; scows and skiffs and prancing horses all in a stained glass sanctuary. I can hear the motorboats, a welcome sound of spring, the whooping fishermen, the hymns the old river still sings for all her children gone.

This is the same old river, the same old wind on autumn nights sing for my Great-Great-Aunt Bia Porter, drifting downstream in her coffin, her long black hair plaited and her face as white as porcelain exposed to the sun, the dead baby in her arms, past home where my Great-Great-Uncle John Nutbeam's horses trotted to the water's edge and stood at attention to watch her pass. She had been John's sweetheart; he deserted her and their baby. This is where Great-Grandfather David worked as a channel-finder for the river boat *Andover* on its Newcastle/Doaktown run. Grandfather Thomas was a log driver and a stunt-man, who practised handsprings on drifting logs. I can still hear him telling us how, one September night, he and Joe Smith, a poet, speared a wagonload of fish at the Salmon Hole to supply a lumber camp for the winter. They burned pitchwood in a wire crew pot, lighting up the water, attracting fish to within reach of the spear. Father worked the log drives, too, at Morse Brook, Black Brook, Cains River, and the Sabies where Uncle Jack Underwood was killed in April 1953 by a log that fell from a landing. They worked the great corporation drives down the main river each year at the end of May. In his own time, Father had seen the river change from a transportation route and food supply to a no-less-important river of recreation.

As a boy, I sat near the schoolhouse door and listened to freedom: blue jays crying in hawthorn trees, the kite-winds of spring, the sparkling river just beyond the rattling flagstaff and the maple leaf flapping its red-and-white nylon threads, luring me from David Copperfield and the War of 1812 until the door, partly open, was closed by the teacher. So many thorns. It seemed summers were longer then; there was more time, more wind, more voices, more river. In the fall of 1958, my brother Win and I jigged school and fished. We landed and my father salted a full barrel of salmon. Now I watch my sons doing abbreviated versions of the same things.

I think now of a time last June when my girlfriend Sally came to visit for a few days. She had a long and stressful drive from the city, and she was exhausted. We built a fire on the ground near the water and roasted trout and sipped wine, listened for the chuckle of loons. The sunset was filled with magic. The following morning we went beneath the hill in front of the camp and planted her flower garden, first thing. Sweet Williams, black-eyed Susans, and salvias. Then we put on our cut-offs, took packsacks and a lunch, and in Father's old boat we drifted until the sun dropped into the horizon. There were long waving strands of eelgrass, while chubs and trout darted away from the boat. Also on the bottom were the long open-mouthed lamprey of June, some dead and some dying as they twisted and rolled on the slime-covered rocks of the eddies, or faced into the currents of the gravel salmon beds. We heard the splash of big fish. Later when the wind came up, we tied a blanket to the canoe pole to fashion a sail and drifted back upstream.

That evening in the cabin as we ate, we heard a frog peep. Then two. Then three. Until the swale was an unbroken litany. In harmony, a toad sang on the river. Wind pushed through the screens to blow out our candles. Sometime in the night during a lightning storm, we exchanged I love yous. It was a great day for so late in the season.

The next morning there was something cool in the wind. Early, when the fog was still on the river, Sally sat with her jaw cupped in her hands, elbows on her bony knees as she scribbled in her diary. Then she had a cup of tea, we embraced, and she was gone, back to her home at The Narrows on the river Saint John. She did not believe in long-running relationships. She had told me many times. I can still feel her rough voice in my ear, the silkiness of her hair, taste the flavour of her breath. She is anything but pretentious, Sally is. And she is a river lover, steadfast, eccentric, and like me not about to change. Now she has taken her place among others, perhaps to return someday in an old song, the rattle of a window, or the fleeting voices that whisper along an eavestroughing. Symbols of freedom, yes, but loneliness too, making it difficult for me to separate mind from matter, love from the illusion of love. Even now, especially now, there is a mystery in all of this that is yet to be solved.

So I'm closing up the books on summer now. I have marked this season of loving you with Os and Xs on my calendar. After so long, you have become the voice of conscience, tradition, and truth. It seems that everyone here is a part of everyone else. River men and river women are poignant, laid-back, lumbering souls with miseries of all kinds. Yet we have a great spirit and a unique love for life.

In the mirror a grey-bearded Zorba the Greek has replaced me. "Old clothes upon a stick to scare a crow," as the poem goes. My tan is fading. Sunshine is fading. Dreams, river, voices in the wind, fading. I am hard of hearing now, hard of sight, hard of logic. And I have no new mythologies. So I sit and watch now as scattered rain drops dimple the river. There is a beaver swimming about with a branch in its teeth. I watch it for a long time. When it submerges, I just sit and watch the river.

My sons, Jeff, Jason, and Steven, who are now part-time river guides, will be coming home for the Thanksgiving weekend. I know they will be here. It is tradition. And they will bring their city girlfriends, tall and willowy young women who have already become my surrogate daughters. I never had a daughter of my own. Perhaps we will have a potluck meal here at Camp Oriole. For sure, on Sunday afternoon the family will get together for a happy hour and a feast at Grandfather's old cabin, just next door to ours. Afterwards, we may take Father and Mother on a drive to the Cains, maybe pick a few wild apples from Great-Grandmother's old trees. (We now use these for baking.) My parents will browse, as they always do, through Great-Grandmother Maggie Porter's old rock cellar. It is hard to find now, and we use an elm tree for a marker because the cellar is really quite grown over with purple-stemmed raspberries, alders, and wild hawthorn trees.

As we talk and look for Gram's currant bushes, we may spook a partridge or a moose bird. Once again Father will marvel and carry to the car some old relic of Gram's. It could be a galvanized teapot with the bottom missing or possibly some pie-shaped pieces of an old dinner plate. Again we will try to piece all this together. Father says he can remember when the house was standing fine, dormant windows and veranda facing the river, and the flat was a field of oats. He and Mother will stand and shake their heads in wonder at what time has done here. Mother will tell us once again how Aunt Bia and her new baby died here, and for a brief moment we will be solemnly caught up in that day. But then we will go to look for cranberries in the old meadows, down where the barns used to be. Maybe some of us will have brought fishing rods and wander off to the river.

WINTER

Lingering Melodies

"I will sing one song for my old Kentucky home." We had stood beside our school desks and sung each Friday afternoon, holding a copy of *The Silver Book of Songs*, an anthology of verse and melodies that included "Swanee River," "O Canada," "The Maple Leaf Forever," and "God Save the Queen." These songs mixed nicely with our dreams of the future, ambitions bigger than life. There had been American influence, yes even then, in the songs and the radio programs. The Lone Ranger and Tonto had been in the schoolyard during lunch hour, and there was a teepee made of poles on the riverbank out back. Inside the classroom a kind of discipline prevailed and there was great tension in our focus on learning. And sometimes, even now, when I hear those old songs, the symbols in them bring back my struggles with long division, the War of Independence, the poetry of Wilfred Campbell. Old school and old home, in the days when my father was still my hero and our little community was the most important place on earth to live.

I think of this now as I walk in my father's fields just as I used to do almost fifty years ago. I am gathering the limbs from an apple tree corpse to burn in the old fireplace. I have come home from Toronto, where I play second violin for the Toronto Symphony Orchestra. My sister, Sara, will arrive from Halifax later today and we will spend Christmas here with the folks. Sara, now a film producer in that city, works very hard. I am sure she will be played out from the drive here, but it will be a nice change of pace for us both. We will have a chance to reminisce; no doubt we will talk on into the night, as we do at such times. Again we will try to fathom it all, look to an ever shortening future and try to put our past into perspective, how we got to where we are. During such talks, I generally have trouble. Because of what time does to memories, it is always hard for me to see my youth clearly. Sometimes Sara will have to set me straight.

However, one part I do remember well is the school I attended for eight years, before I went into grade nine, before the buses came and took us to the big regional academy in the city. This and a teacher whose name was Catherine Green, a young woman who influenced my life. I think of her now as I approach the old school grounds.

As an adolescent I had hated school. I would sit inside the schoolhouse door and listen to freedom: blue jays crying in hawthorn trees, crickets singing in the playground wildflowers, vagabond winds rattling against a slanting flagstaff. When I hunted partridge in the black alder swamps, where I would steal away whenever possible, the wind carried the sweet incense of autumn: the smoke of bonfires, the lure of river and woods, the crack of deer rifles, the smell of decaying leaves under my rubbers. Even now a series of images repeat themselves inside me, each from a different person, a different place, and of course a different state of mind. They live on in the old school songs and poetry like coals in the ashes of burnt out fantasies.

Along the line of smoky hills/the crimson forest stands... Indian Summer, a poem by Wilfred Campbell. I remember reciting this, standing by my school desk, glancing out the window to watch the early winter come down, wishing I were somewhere else. By the end of October, our clocks had been set back and darkness came early. The autumn rains slanted across bleached fields already frozen, the brooks and the river also frozen over. Then came the snow. At first only a little, like salt. Tiny pellets lay in dead leaves and on trays of ice along the roadway as my sister and I walked to school. It dusted about with the wind from passing vehicles and mixed with blowing sand to look like ashes. In the woods behind the school, snow zigzagged among trees to catch and hold on boughs and leave bare patches of frozen moss. It turned our cardboard teepee into porcelain, froze our boot-tracks into china saucers. But this inspired a new exuberance in us because, by the end of November, Miss Green had started rehearsing her Christmas program, which we regarded as a break from schoolwork.

At home I had put in my order to Santa for a new jackknife, but this gift was uncertain. Our parents spoke of the hardships of past winters. They cautioned us children that it would be cruel to expect much because times were bad. So, as the Christmas season approached, windbreaks and snow fences were erected, our house banked and shuttered. Our dreams we adjusted many times, selfish wants relinquished to dire needs to optional practicalities (if things went right), and these simple necessities were to be shared equally by brothers and sisters.

This was the time in our lives when Christmas brought a lot of magic. Everything that we had encountered since Halloween would have been a part of the Yuletide season. The woods suddenly became scattered with little red berries and pine buds, the trees had taken on a new shade of silver, a stronger scent of balsam, and the frozen river had become a place to test our hand-me-down skates. Even the old schoolhouse and our teacher Miss Green grasped the spirit.

My mother and Sara, who was in grade four, sat by the piano in the living room and sang "O Christmas Tree," a song which my sister had been rehearsing for the school concert. Our mother was "not well" that year and would not be coming to the program. She would have a new baby in February.

Our school was a one-room clapboard building with a porch, three long windows down the side, a black weathered woodshed, and two backhouses (Girls and Boys), which stood among hawthorn trees at the edge of the playground. The schoolhouse was heated by a sowbellied wood stove with the words "Enterprise Foundries–Sackville New Brunswick," cast in the shape of a horseshoe on the door.

Miss Green, a tall, willowy, and delicate-looking blond, appeared quite stiff, and she seldom smiled. Her big brown eyes were easily made tearful—I am guilty of having made her cry—and during study periods she sighed a lot. She was in her early twenties (although she seemed much older to us then), convent-educated and teaching here on a local licence. She was paying for room and board at the old McLaren Farm next to ours. She had come from the southern part of the province, a brooding town woman who had not been accepted in our community. There was mystery about her past and a lot of gossip.

"She plays that long-haired stuff on the fiddle. It's certainly not the kind of music that anyone around here can stand," I heard Mrs. Crumb once say in my father's store. "Or 'violin' as she calls it."

"I never could see where she was all that good-looking, either," Mr. Porter added and winked at my father as he spit tobacco juice into a tin can.

Because I was big for my age, I stood awkwardly among the smaller children. We sang the school songs and recited allegiance to our flag, which was held by two clothespins on a string. Some days there were only seven or eight of us in school. I was in charge of tending fires, so I had to be there early. I also carried water from a brook under the hill and kept the doorstep shovelled, as well as a pathway to the outhouses and woodshed. For these chores I received free violin lessons from Miss Green, one night a week at her boarding house. Everyone else my age was working in the woods.

At school, Miss Green was very strict. We were not allowed to whisper or smile or glance out the windows. If she caught us at any of these things, she stood us facing into the corner for a long time. Sometimes we got the strap, which she kept in her desk drawer beneath a rainbow chocolate box containing pencils, erasers, paper clips, and elastic bands. Miss Green appeared to be cold all the time and sat with her feet up on the stove. Occasionally, she would ask me to go to the shed for firewood. Once I spilled an armload of kindling, pretending to trip and fall as I came through the door. Chunks scattered into the aisles. The other kids laughed. Miss Green looked at me with great disgust. Yet I had done this, not to provoke the teacher, but as a respite against the relentless afternoon. As I gathered up the sticks, embarrassed, I realized my stunt was not funny.

On a sunless day in late November, all day Miss Green sat, staring off into space, with her coat on and her feet up on the stove. The next day she was ill, and there was no school. She was laid up for almost two weeks. It was rumoured at the local store that she was expecting. Some said she already had a baby, whom she gave away. Others said her baby was born dead and was burned in the big stove at the foot of the McLaren's stairs. That, or it had been buried under the doorstep. Of course, there was no baby.

When Miss Green was back in school, the gossip turned to excessive discipline because she kept some of us late to work out long division when we were needed at home to do our evening chores. But by then we were well into rehearsing recitations, songs, and dialogues for the Christmas program. The girls had drawn little holly leaves and berries with coloured chalk around the edge of the blackboard. Crayoned drawings hung in windows. The school had been thoroughly scrubbed and smelled of disinfectant and new stove polish. Because I was the biggest I had been sent to the swamp for a Christmas tree, a tree which, according to the class, was too tall and open. Miss Green said I should have gone to more open woods, where a tree would have room to reach out. But we decorated this tree with haws, rosehip berries, strings of frozen cranberries we had gathered from the swamp, and our gifts for the teacher. I did not have a present for Miss Green, so I wrapped the wool mittens my mother had knit for me and put them on the tree. I later told my mother I had lost them.

Before the program, our school was filled with magic. I carried chairs from around the community, filling the aisles and the back of the classroom. During lunch, our teacher had gone home and put on a new black dress, red sweater, and long beads. She looked very nice, but even in that dress there was a sternness about her that kept us all on our guard. She had also brought her violin case, which she stood in the corner. She intended to play a Christmas number for the parents.

There was a light wind, and it was snowing softly as we sat and waited for members of the community. Miss Catherine Green paced the floor. Her delicate fingers played with her beads in a kind of prayer. She stopped only to look, preoccupied, out the window, past the crayoned Santas into the fading light and the stretch of road that led to the schoolhouse. She often stared that way, like she couldn't see the obvious. I had come to regard her with a feeling of defensiveness as if I had secretly taken her side in things. I could feel that she had sensed this in me because she often spared me the hard questions. A bond grew, ever so fragile, like an antique Christmas decoration.

The afternoon was hurrying past to defy us all. And no one was coming. At quarter to three Miss Green decided to go ahead with the program.

I struggled within my adolescent timidity amid giggles as I recited in front of the class, who had heard it a hundred times, and a dozen empty chairs:

Away up in the rocky north
Where Christmas trees won't grow
All snug and cosy in his bed
Lives a little Eskimo.
His tiny stockings and mukluks
He hangs up by the fire
He lives so close to Santa Claus
The reindeer never tire.

I took a bow and sat down. There was applause—not for me, but for the liberty of making a noise here. The five schoolgirls, my sister Sara among them, stood in a row at the front of the room and sang, "Santa Claus is coming, we will welcome him with glee, we'll hang a gift for everyone upon our Christmas tree...hurrah, hurrah." With each "hurrah" their hands made a sweeping gesture as if to grab something invisible. They bowed together and went to their seats. Then I went outside and stood in the cold entryway. On cue, I knocked and came in, a beggar in search of a remedy for my aching back. I rolled on the schoolhouse floor, moaning and gasping. Pockets of laughter broke out. Even our teacher, who seemed to have no time for folly, offered a piteous half-smile.

As I gathered the chairs after the program, Miss Green, sitting at her desk, took a handkerchief from her sleeve. She wiped her nose and dabbed her soft brown eyes.

"Christmastime," she sobbed, "I thought some of the parents just might come..."

The next day, snow puffed off roofs and drifted into dooryards to make cliffs in the lee of buildings. Flower pots that sat on open verandas became tubs of ice cream. Fence posts became frosted popsicles and our field's shaggy spruce grew into giant silver bells as we gathered the dead limbs of apple trees and carried them home for the hearth fire. Our parents made much ado about Santa coming down the chimney and keeping his suit clean of the black ash. I can still remember the restless night that followed: the turkey, the church service, the visits from neighbours.

Then suddenly, amid all the singing, fairy tales, storm fear, and hearth fires, as though the whole event had been executed by the hands of a magician, Christmas came and went, almost without us seeing it happen. It was like reality had gobbled up our pre-Christmas illusions—everything we had looked forward to for months was over in a matter of hours. Cap guns and plastic-face cotton dolls with tilting blue eyes, the red fire engines and twisted candy canes lay scattered in a haze of tinselled rejections, selfish desires, and false hopes. Disillusioned with ourselves, with each other, and with our parents, we were left trying to adjust back into the harsh world of winter. In January we pondered the obscure poems of Sir Charles G. D. Roberts and Robert Frost. *Whose woods these are I think I know.* Frost's "Stopping by Woods on a Snowy Evening" is still a favourite.

One afternoon, while working out our long division on the blackboard, Miss Green confronted me about carving my initials in a heart next to hers on the door of the girl's outhouse. She said she had seen it during lunch-hour and recognized my printing. She knew about the pocket-knife I had received for Christmas.

"My brother William did it when he was home from the woods for the holidays!" I pleaded to her, stone-faced in front of the class.

"Don't you lie to me Scott Millen!" she yelled and tugged my sleeve to march me into the porch so the others couldn't see. The blistering strap fell upon my hands and Miss Green's eyes filled with tears. It was like she was being punished for her indifference, or that she needed to vent her grievance with the community against one of us. I grabbed the strap, threw it on the floor, and ran for home. I think now that I did this to help spare her the moment. I knew I had pushed her to wield the strap, and I was sorry.

In the evening my mother made me go to the teacher's boarding house to apologize to Miss Green for carving the initials, lying about it, and running away. I can remember standing nervously in the McLaren's parlour, my cap in my hands.

"Miss Green, I'm so sorry about what happened there today in school," I said. "It was a terrible thing I did."

At this she smiled and squeezed my arm. She said that neither of us should ever mention the incident again.

Toward spring my mother invited Miss Green to our house for supper. It was a sunny evening when she walked up the highway from her boarding house; the wind caught her scarf and the skirts of her long brown coat as she proudly carried her violin case. She sat in the kitchen rocker and talked to my mother in her refined schoolteacher's voice. We ate in the dining room that night and everyone was polite. After the meal, my mother asked her to play.

Miss Catherine Green stood in the centre of the parlour with sheet music on a stand and tapped her foot up and down. Her long hair shone beneath the electric lights as she played. She handled the polished instrument so delicately, holding it to her chin as though it was a part of her soul while she played with four quick, lithe fingers. Everyone in our house could see that Miss Green had a lot of class. She performed the kind of music that none of us except my mother (who could play by ear) really understood or appreciated. Until then we had heard it only on the radio. She played the theme from the radio show *The Lone Ranger*—William Tell's Overture in B-flat—and Tara's theme, which I didn't know at the time was from the motion picture *Gone With the Wind*. Miss Green's music filled the room with images well beyond the physical and metaphoric borders of our small community. She seemed pleased when we applauded, blushing openly as she put her instrument back in its case. I knew then I wanted to learn to play that kind of music. My new fantasy was more real than any of the others. I worked hard at my music after that night.

In March Miss Green was sick again, and for a time Mr. McLaren drove her to school in his old square-top car. Then the school was closed and a letter was sent to homes saying that the teacher was suffering from tuberculosis and the doctor was admitting her to the sanatorium in St. John. No grades were given at our school that year.

From her bed at the sanatorium, Catherine Green exchanged letters with my mother. Once she sent a black-and-white photo of herself propped up with pillows against her runged bedstead. She always asked how I was doing in school and if I was keeping up with my music. Sometime later she wrote to say that she was getting married to a young doctor. We never heard from Catherine Green again.

I think of her now as I walk through the old orchard to what used to be our open fields. The ground is damp and brown. Dark clouds appear to be holding up the snow. It seems like every practical thing from those days has fallen down and blown away. The stems of ragged cattails have buckled, the rosehip and the hawthorn have withered and decayed, and a new growth of shrub has infested my father's farm. Where the schoolhouse once stood there is now only a clearing, the abandoned sheds having burned, the classroom moved for use as a machine shed by a neighbour. Only the girl's outhouse remains. It stands on the site, slanting and forlorn. I walk over and check its door, but the scars of my youth have long since grown over. I think of Catherine Green and I try to grasp some of the spirit of that faded day, when a pretty blond woman played the violin for my family. The memory dances like a distorted video but brightens now with a drifting flake of snow and the lingering melody of an old school song.

At the Grand Hotel

"We're a long way from Cedar Swamp tonight," Angela chuckled.

"Yeah, if they could see us now!" Johnny had a brief image of his old cabin sitting empty on a riverbank in the northeast of New Brunswick. Usually on winter Saturday nights, he would be there, alone, having a rum and Coke and watching the hockey game on television. It had been like that since Amanda left him thirty-odd years ago. Since then, he had gone back to enjoying the companionship of old school friends. They sometimes met down at the Waverley for coffee. Once in a while they played darts over at the legion on Tuesday nights.

For a long time Johnny Long had stewed over travelling to Europe alone, especially getting around in the big cities. So Angela, his sister from Montreal, had agreed to go with him. The trip had been part of his seasonal job as a river guide. He had been invited to come and work at the Expo in Bern. For a week he had stood in the booth as a kind of river mascot, and even though he couldn't speak the language he had enjoyed every minute. Already, the trip was coming to an end, just when he was starting to gain a little confidence.

It was snowing in Interlaken, and there were few people on the streets as Johnny and Angela walked. Only the occasional whistle of a far-off mountain train or the distant cannon-fire of avalanche-starters broke the silence. The wood shutters on many of the chalet-style buildings were already closed, the working rich in bed. In the week they'd been there, Johnny had grown to love the stone city with its rugged beauty, excellent food, music, and most of all the wonderful people. He and Angela had been told that in summer there, tourists out-number residents five to one. Now it was a quiet hamlet tucked beneath looming mountains, with many of its novelty shops and sixty-odd hotels closed.

They had been to the Lord Byron and had watched a tall, matronly woman in traditional mountaineer costume play the accordion and yodel. She told them she had once been the champion yodeller in Switzerland and had represented her country in the opening ceremonies at the winter Olympics in Sarajevo. Johnny and Angela now walked past a street vendor roasting chestnuts toward a big café with a tree growing up through its veranda roof and out in the direction of the open Ora, a tributary of the Rhine. As they followed the sidewalk, snow crunched under their feet. At the train station, a square-front electric engine and lighted coaches sat on the tracks. The passengers inside wore colourful clothes and carried the rucksacks of skiers. These people, they were told, were on their way from Zürich and Bern, heading to the Alpine region of Austria.

Johnny and his sister walked along a cobbled alley to where the street ended at the foot of the mountains, which looked spooky in the dark with the snow coming down off them. They passed the park with its big bare trees and roosting pigeons and the snow-laden benches under them. The two-tier bandstand in the centre, like the ornate old buildings in the local business district, was covered with snow. They finally reached the Grand Hotel, the town's largest and most elegant. As they passed an open window, Johnny could hear a violin, the mellow strains of "Twilight Time." Having a flair for fiddle music, he insisted on stepping inside.

In the lobby, the modest Christmas decorations were still in place. In the centre of the foyer stood a droopy mountain spruce with gold stars, brass horns, and rolls of sheet music tied up in bows.

Little white lights were strung on the limbs, as they were on the wrought-iron balconies outside. Sculptures and paintings reflected on the polished black and silver floor. A huge chandelier hung on chains from a glass dome, which revealed the mountains with trees up halfway and the white cliffs beyond, which were more beautiful during a sunset.

"We're sure as hell not lookin' out at Cedar Swamp tonight," Angela said and pinched her brother's arm. "I hope you don't mind me saying that."

"No, no. Not likely. Say what ya like. You came from there yourself didn't you? Only I'm still there, and proud to be. No, I don't give a shit. And I don't care who does. We can't change where we come from. I can't anyway."

"Now, now. Let's not get all flustered."

"Who's getting flustered?" Johnny wiped his glasses and then blew his nose into the handkerchief.

They followed the music into the candle-lit lounge with the assistance of a host and sat by a wood table at the back of the dark panelled barroom, which was warm and cheerful. A waiter in uniform brought them a beverage menu and miniature flashlights to read by.

"We'll order just a small bottle…maybe wine," Angela said as they scanned the list for a vintage they could afford. The most expensive bottle was 150 francs. They were obviously paying for the dancing girls who would appear later. (There was a bigger bar across the hall where they could hear laughter.)

"What the hell!" Johnny said. "I'm buying a big bottle of that dry sherry."

"That's the spirit!"

Waiting for the wine, they listened to a violinist who introduced herself as Monique. Her brother, Kurt, was accompanying her on the Spanish guitar. Monique was thirty-fiveish with long raven hair, high cheekbones, and large sensitive eyes. Her white silk dress revealed a slim frame. She smiled and winked at Johnny when the waiter gave her his twenty francs with a request for the "I-talian Waltz." She stood with one foot resting upon the bottom rung of a stool. At a glance she was assembled from the best fragments of Greek sculpture. She smiled again, and her natural, slightly uneven teeth made her real. The music was tender and mystical. Johnny Long closed his eyes, absorbing it slowly like the wine, and it was as if he were skiing down the great Jungfrau in the dark. There was no one else in the room but Monique and Johnny then, no one else in the world. She was probably the most beautiful woman he had ever seen, and now they were being pulled together in the music by a chorus of invisible strings.

Looking at Monique, Johnny Long knew that all of the women who moved him in this way had somehow looked alike. At the very least they all had dark riveting eyes. Would there be something to build on here this time? He knew that the women he may have pursued as a younger man he could now only look upon with envy and a sense of loss. He felt he had grown too old, really, and that if such a woman noticed him it would be for the wrong reasons. He was seventy-two years old. When he thought of himself in this way, he felt very sad. He wished he could trade himself for a younger man, even a reckless, no good son-of-a-bitch, but younger. Because youth was when everything exciting happened to a man. Still, he smiled at Monique. When their eyes met he raised his glass and winked at her.

Now she played music that Johnny had heard only in dreams, deep in some lonely moment of sleep. It was like the sweetness was coming not from the instrument but from somewhere within this woman. Like she was extending herself in it and he was drifting, as if on a river, sometimes rapidly, sometimes slowly. She seemed to be asking, How does it feel? Is it good for you this way or that? And she stared at Johnny with those dark gypsy eyes and played on.

Johnny was with Monique, on the train, travelling through the winter mountains around the Thundersee, past Darligen, Leissigen, and Krattigen along the river, still open now in mid-January, to Bern. They were strolling down the wide cobbled streets, visiting bear pits and outdoor markets, tasting the flavour of roasted chestnuts, visiting the dinner theatre at the ancient wine-cellar, where she sat across from him at the table sipping schnapps, eyes sparkling in the candlelight, her hearty but innocent laugh attracting attention.

There was a pause in the music. Johnny and his sister applauded. Angela whispered in his hear, "But wouldn't you like to do it to her?"

"I'd stay with her awhile anyway. Ha, ha, ha."

Then Monique played the "Emperor Waltz" by Strauss, and Johnny was on the river again.

The cog train was carrying them up the hundred-year-old tracks to the Jungfrau region at the top of Europe through the windswept mountain village of Allmend to Egergletscher, where they would lunch at the outdoor café and bask in the hot winter sun in the lee of the peaks with all the colourful young people around them. Then they would go through tunnels to Wengwald where they would ski the slopes toward Interlaken with its green lakes, a postcard in the distance, to the Ora which flows smooth and green behind the hotel.

He thought then, It would be enough just to be with her anywhere and not do anything. For an instant Johnny Long remembered home: Cedar Swamp Road, his empty cabin on the river, the dreaded hollow weekends, the hockey game, the rum that masked his loneliness. Could this really happen to him now? For a long time he had hung on to a dream. He had tried to love someone who no longer existed. Then he had tried to pursue love again, at first without hope, then without youth. Now, finally, there was someone to stir the ashes, a chemistry he had not experienced in years that was as close to anything he had felt in a long time to being accepted. The other times were illusory feelings he had found with phantom lovers grasped in dreams.

He thought of his friends back home on the river and wondered what they would think of him if he took the beautiful Monique home with him. *Boys did anyone see the woman Johnny Long brought home from overseas. They say she's not bad lookin' but can't speak a word of English. Plays that fancy music on the fiddle. Good fiddler himself, Johnny, one time, before he started drinkin'.* If only he could win her heart he would take her there, show her off, show them all a thing or two.

At the break, because there was no one else in the bar, Monique and Kurt came to their table and asked to sit with them. Johnny offered to buy drinks.

"Yah-yah. Schnapps. Dunka, merci, sank you," Monique said, adding, "When I see you come in, I want to come by you right away. The sitiaition is I sink I could know you from before, sometimes. Do you sink so? We don't meet maybe in the last time?" She laughed at herself. "I don't sink my English is no good!" She was looking into Johnny's eyes.

"It's a heckofa lot better than my German!" Johnny laughed. "But I don't think we ever met. I know I'd remember you Marie."

"Monique."

"Monique, Monique, right! Don't mind me. I'm hard of hearing."

They raised and clinked their glasses. Everyone said cheers in sequence.

"Cheers." Monique smiled and tossed her hair aside before sipping her drink. Then she lit a cigarette and made a tiny smoke ring with her lips.

With Monique sitting beside him, Johnny had become the man he had always wished he could be. He had a brief image of his small circle of friends playing darts at the legion in Cedar Swamp as he walked in with this woman on his arm.

On impulse he said, "Monique let me try yer fiddle!"

Monique carefully passed the violin over the drinks to Johnny and in his sudden provincial squeamishness, he was sorry he had asked. He felt everyone's gaze on him and he sweated as he squeaked out "Come Listen to the Mockingbird," a poem from an inarticulate man. Yet somehow Johnny felt this was okay with Monique, that she was genuine and would accept his music because now she had put her hand on his shoulder.

"Yah-yah. I sink so you play some too!" she said and laughed. Trembling, Johnny quickly passed the instrument back into the hands in which it belonged.

He wanted someone who would be able to love him just the way he was. He suddenly believed that it could be Monique, even though he had learned from experience that the illusion of perfection came only with newness. He would have her beside him while it was still good because he knew that she would never be this perfect again, except when he looked back after memory had distorted her.

"You are Americans? I sink so?"

"No, no. We…are…from…Canada." Angela said, exaggerating each word.

"Yah-yah. Canada. I sink so, I go by you in the next times, next summer. Maybe Tor-ron-to."

"Great! When you're over there maybe we can…" Johnny had a quick image of Monique visiting his house in Cedar Swamp.

Johnny Long held his gaze on Monique as she told Angela she had studied violin since she was five and the instrument had cost her mother twenty thousand francs many years ago. Monique told Angela that her favourite composers were J. S. Bach, Antonio Vivaldi, Jerome Kern, and Stephen Capilli. Johnny scribbled his name and address on a serviette. She said she would mail him a CD of her music.

"Look, maybe we could be pen pals, keep in touch that way until you come to Canada." Johnny was straining not to offer her more. "I would like to write to you once in a while."

"Yah-yah. I like that if you can. It was good for me to. But I sink the sitiaition is from before, it's like I know you." She rested her arm on his back this time. "It is like that for you too I sink?"

"Oh yes, yes I certainly feel the same way!" Johnny raised up on the chair. "It's like we're old flames getting to know each other all over again." And then he hollered, "Waiter! Bring us another round here, will you?" He put his arm around Monique as if he were going to pull her close, and everyone in the room laughed.

"He…likes…to…write…letters. Johnny…will…write…to…you," Angela made motions, reassuring Monique. Then to Kurt, "my…brother…likes…to…write…tell…your…sister."

"Please, Angela, let me do my own talking. For once just let me handle something myself will you!" Johnny had turned on his chair. "Look, Monique, maybe we could be more than just friends!"

"Johnny!" Angela said and tugged his sleeve.

"No, no! Now you just leave me alone here, please."

Monique smiled but did not say anything.

Johnny knew she could see that he was feeling something for her because she became coy. She held the violin against her breast as her gaze shifted about the room. She drew on the cigarette and blew smoke toward the ceiling. But she did not speak, and her silence stabbed at Johnny because he knew she had heard what he said and that she had time to respond. He had experienced this awkwardness before. He knew what she was thinking, and it wasn't at all in his favour. He continued to smile as though he did not notice these subtleties, pretending that he was still in the game and that it was all merely playful pursuit for the benefit of her ego and his own. He said, "I love violin music, 'specially if it's played by a beautiful woman," and chuckled. Johnny sensed that Monique was embarrassed for him because she had started talking loudly without saying much. He could always feel the rejection long before a woman ever said anything to him. It was a kind of sixth sense that he had developed from experience. He thought, I'm really a good lad but she wouldn't know that because she hasn't taken time to look deep. She would have to know me to reject me. And he felt some better about himself. He always allowed himself a little boost to rationalize this kind of hurt.

Now Monique was smiling in her vibrant way as her brother reached across the table and tugged her sleeve, "Wir müssen wieder arbeiten. Dieser alte Dussel verliebt sich in dich." They excused themselves politely and returned to the stage.

"In love Johnny?" Angela teased in Monique's accent. "I sink so. Good for you, too. Maybe the next times I come to see you in Can-a-da?"

"Oh shut up Angela!"

There was a time when Johnny Long could drink wine all evening and never feel it, but tonight he had suddenly become tired as though the wine was dragging him down instead of picking him up. He felt irritable and his head ached and his insides burned down deep in the pit of his stomach. Maybe they should get a taxi back to their room.

"Sir, your drink. How is your drink, sir?" The waiter was loud in Johnny's ear, just as the music, a different violin now, started to play again.

"What's that? Who? Oh yes. No, thank you. Danka. It's okay. It's a wonderful place here. Nice people. Vielen dank."

"No, we have to go," Angela said to the waiter. She turned to Johnny, "We really have to go. We have that early flight, remember?"

Johnny glanced at his watch as he stood up. "Wait a minute. I have to talk to Monique." There were still things he wanted to say.

Monique spotted them leaving and came down from the stage. She hugged them and gave each one a traditional kiss on the cheek.

"Ciao." The empty ciao. The lifeless hug.

"Look Monique maybe we could..." She had already turned and was walking back onto the stage.

Johnny and Angela fumbled with their coats, scarves, and gloves, bundling up against the stinging little scuds of snow that were coming down off the mountains and puffing off the roofs and would take their breath away as they walked. Angela paid the bill with travellers' cheques and waited for the change.

Two big men elbowed past them and stood near the stage to listen to the violin. They were dressed in mountaineer clothing and had been singing the rowdy songs of the sheep herders whose farms were now buried beneath metres of snow in the mountains above them. Johnny and Angela had seen these men at the Lord Byron and had left there because of the racket they were making. The bartender there had threatened to throw them all out. They were Americans trying to fit into the local scene, which they did not seem to know was a quiet one. They drew up chairs and ordered a bottle of twenty-eight-year-old Scotch. It must have cost them plenty. Johnny watched as Monique and her brother approached their table.

"When I see you come in, I want to come by you right away," Monique said. "Do you sink, we meet maybe sometimes before?"

Board Ice

It is a breezy mid-October noon. We have been here since early morning. There is a dullness in the air, so I have built a fire to lighten the day. I stand beside the blaze and watch my clients fishing the rapids. There is McGill, Findlay, Scaling, and Taylor. Having waded out into the chest-deep water, they look like busts of the rich and famous that stand in town squares. Between them and me, wedges of granite emerge from the water: the backs of rhinos, oddly shaped pyramids, and miniature castles, draped now with veils of purple seaweed. All the leaves have fallen, and dead rushes stick out of eddies like quills from trays of ink. A Canada jay chirps its little song, *tweet-tweet*, as a light breeze catches the river to make a silver patchwork of lace, a design for embroidery. And there are chunks of foam adrift: snowflakes, doilies, and fists of lamb's wool. My smoke drifts in a haze and makes a cocoon over the water. The air has prominent hollow sounds now before the rain. Out in the main stream, fish are jumping to nourish the interest of the men and make them shout at one another in accented monotones before settling down to fish again.

 I huddle in reflection, going over some old poems I have read and now realize I must read again. The works trigger deeper and more meaningful images for me now: April as the cruellest month, the gathering of rosebuds, the tiring of the great harvest, and the queen of far-away all leave me contemplative on this wintry day. Familiar lines to re-read, reinterpret. You see, I have been a man of books, a man of images, an inside man. I have spent most of my life working on that part of myself. Now, at seventy-eight, I pride myself on the comfort I find in it. An old mind following old lines I once thought I understood, lines that have taken on new meanings. I shield myself in this kind of meditation because it is so much warmer on the inside, for me.

Since you have gone (so long ago), because you have gone, this is the only way I can find a small measure of comfort. To those on the outside I have become tiresome, a bore. I am poorly dressed and my ragged hair has threads of grey, which can be frightening, especially to the young who play out here on days like this. Today I am congested from the dampness. My knees and ankles ache from climbing slippery shores and wading among the bull rushes all this fall. I cannot stand nor lay nor sit in comfort anymore. I long for genuine conversation, good food, beautiful music, and real friends. The friends I search for inside myself because many of them have already gone, so that here on the darkening shores there is at least some light. For there is nowhere on earth as hollow and chilling as a river after all the leaves have come down and winter is approaching. Dark and blustery winter. The hollow, silent old river, a stream that flows from out of a rocky past toward an uncertain end. Perhaps a small fire will take some of the storm fear out of this day, I think. A cup of tea. There are echoes in the hollow air as I gather spruce limbs and pine sticks that look like chicken bones to add to the blaze. To get my little fire going I have burned the index pages of Plato's *Republic* (but have savoured the sonnets of Shakespeare and Shelley, because I always see you somewhere in them).

With aching hands I have whittled a green sapling for a hanging stick and, for a teapot, I have fashioned a two-litre tin pail burnt black, with a handle twisted from wire. Having filled the pail with water from the brook, I hang it over the fire to boil. I sit on a rock and watch the water steam as the orange flames lick the base of the can to make it sing, then whistle and dance. As I feed more sticks under the pail, the flames snap and crack, sending smoke and cinders out over the river.

Finally, the water in the can begins to bubble in dancing bulbs of blown glass that splatter onto the flame, making it spit and sputter and puff. I fumble in the box-lunch for tea, Earl Grey, and toss three or four bags into the water to make an amber hiss and gurgle before using clawlike hands to lift the tea and set it on a flat rock to steep and cool. (If it cools too quickly it will discolour the flavour.) It starts to rain softly, dimpling the tea and the river that is more smooth now because the wind has gone down.

I fumble through my packsack for my old blue raincoat. Carefully, I wade out into the stream where they can hear me above the din of rapids, and I shout, "Tea time." Then I struggle back to the fireside, my comfort zone. I build up the blaze, arrange tin mugs on a ledge, and set out brandy which we use for sweetener, along with the cream they use to soften the taste.

The fishers wander in, one at a time. They stand around and take off their gloves to hold their red and eager hands and their rubber boots to the fire, until their felt soles begin to smell. They remark about the coolness here in Canada so early in the autumn. They talk of the fish they have seen in these pools on cool days like this and the fish they have risen on such-and-such a fly on this kind of day, in this kind of water. And they reminisce about previous trips—the ducks, deer, and bear they have killed in our country and in others on days just like this. And they speak of what a break they are having, away from their offices and away from their spouses, but they regret missing the ball scores and the results of trading on the stock exchange. They wonder if any new money has come in since they have left home. Still, they want to stretch the day into the night. For they are really nature lovers, woods people, they say.

McGill has a plan. He says he is going to poison all the coyotes in his province to help save the deer for the hunting season. *Dip wieners into gasoline and set them out on the low branches of trees.* Findlay is going to shoot all the ducks to help protect the fish. *Blast the hell out of every last one.* And Scaling is going to donate some money to the popular restoration groups, who will replenish the streams with tank fish so the fishing will be better down the road. Taylor says the whole problem is that there are too few trees in the woods. McGill thinks we have too many old-growth trees that consume the water, and this is why our rivers are getting smaller each year. They argue this point. Scaling thinks there should be more plantations, more uniform woods, perhaps all pine trees.

The men boast to each other about the great schools they attended and the alumni reunions coming up. They compare the great commencement speeches they have heard. Suddenly it is raining so hard that the stream is frosted over like crisper glass and I cannot see for the fog. As the rain comes straight down like weighted twines, it collects on the shoulders of my raincoat, which begins to leak. Water streams down my neck. I pour the tea and offer a dash of brandy. They huddle to light their cigars from a twig held to the fire, then sip the steaming brew and talk in barks, laughing in sharp staccato bursts. They crowd each other to make room around the fire, room for themselves in the conversation, like children in front of an ice cream wagon. As the rain falls, it cools their tea and their cigars disintegrate and the ashes fall into the tin mugs. They move under a tree to keep the spirit alive, the spirit of this kind of day—a day that I have long since tried to block out.

After being on the river so long, I have lost track of what day it really is. Is it Saturday or Sunday? At my age every day is Sunday, especially here on the river. Is this really the new age? And what stream is this? "s there still a stream, a country for me? Every day now seems to have a strange origin, and I struggle for the spirit of a familiar place. I was once an outdoor person myself. But I know this can never be again. To go back is impossible, lest I go inside to where life is glorified by the changes that growth brings to a thing. Many my age are in this place that is forever beckoning to me now.

When the tea is almost gone, my guests slosh what is left onto the rocks, grab their tackle, and head out into the river to jostle for position and start over. A Canada jay glides down on silent wings and tilts its little head in question, its eyes beads of glass. Having gained my trust, it hops up to me and I serve it crumbs like the Eucharist. Then I build up the fire, pour what tea is left into my cup, and turn my back to the river to look for shelter somewhere beneath the hemlock, to a place where I won't see this day for what it has become.

My internal images reappear in new dreams, and the seasons that have long since gone come back to me. Nourished and guided in retrospect, they dance in a way that pleases *me* this time. Old enemies reconcile in a haze of memory, repaying me their debts with showers of accolades. They burn bright for a time, even glow, as if infused with a sudden impulse to care. And I embrace them, in a sense. The flames smoulder but twinkle in the rain as the smoke forms a cloud over the water and drifts upstream. I follow the images through the cruel rains of April and the lightning storms of summer to sometime after harvest, to this winter's day. Oh, it's just some kind of childish game I like to play. There is always new hope in a child, and that inner child in me is still full of energy and dreams.

I am very young, and once again the ice has begun to freeze along the shoreline bushes. "Board ice," my father calls it. A grey sky is closing down and snow is in the wind, already. Soon it will be scudding from out of the north to make patches of white on a slate scrolled by the blades of skates. Down forms in my eyes, a yellow and foggy fleece that is mesmerizing, and I am not sure which way to turn. I know it is Saturday morning and I am looking for the ice, my sister and brother and I. Oxhana and Harold are coming down to join us. Everything is sparkling against the bright sunlight. Slipping and sliding, we are moving through the bent grass that crunches under our feet like frozen moss, leaving our tracks to dry and warm against the morning sun, making black footprints to be followed days and weeks later. The hawthorn berries have fallen, and the sun no longer warms us.

The first signs are the beads. We all notice the glass-like beads along the water's edge—frozen teardrops that have formed overnight in ragged grass. These beads glitter like a network of crystals with stems, brittle to the touch, between a river of iced tea and the strawlike shore grass that's standing upright because we haven't had real snow yet. We step on straw-lined test tubes and they snap. These test tubes and frozen teardrops melt and moisten the sand as the day warms, so that the shore is bare and dry again before dusk. Then the cycle repeats itself, slightly stronger each chilly morning that we come to the river to look for ice, treading along in mindless banter.

Until one Saturday we find, in the unmoving shallows beneath the rushes, a plate of glass over the eddy. Strong and complete, frosted glass as thin as cellophane in places, and thick as the smoky plastic used to cover our windows for winter. We jump on it to test its strength against rubber heels. We take off our mittens and pick up the angled pieces to look through them, first at the shadowy trees, then at the smaller, embroidered port plates that have formed overnight and move past to make a black-and-white conclave farther out. We stare at these and listen to them shhhhing and bumping against one another, crowding into the channel in a reluctant yet hurried migration. Their edges have become furrowed and scalloped into fancy pie plates, until against the sun they grow apart as clear as moving pictures of the washed gravel beneath them. The pieces we are holding melt and drip on our sleeves, and we let them fall and break. A Saturday ritual.

There are snow flurries scattered in the wind when, on a morning in December, we test the board ice once again—first by throwing rocks, then by dropping a log. Would it be strong enough to skate on? Not near the outer edge, of course, but in the eddy itself we think it is. There has been no autumn rains so the water had not risen. And we know what is under the river ice, here. We know the river will freeze across soon because it really is winter now. Any sooner would have been bad luck, for if it freezes across in November, according to our parents, it is certain to go out again and make a helluva mess.

We watch the board ice thicken, watch the powdery bottom grow lifeless beneath it and the tiny fish disappear and the waving eelgrass fade to black strings of twine. The plates that move past grow bigger and bigger and move more slowly, until the whole concern is a world of moving craters. We know it will stop one night and freeze solid. Then, after a day or two, someone will pick their way across for the first time, and with the axe put the tiny bushes in a staggered row for us to follow.

Finally, seeing that the board ice is strong in close, we run home for our skates and return to the shore, out of breath. We sit on mittens placed on flat boulders along the shore to tie our skates. Then stand on unsure ankles, our unsure young selves. Using a twisted tree branch for support, we move about in small circles. We begin in straight lines, then zigzag to chase one another. We bump and fall down and get up to try again. We scream and laugh so that our fathers and mothers can hear us from our homes. We gather alder skeletons from the hillside and build our Saturday bonfire. With the heel of a discarded rubber boot and some tree branches, we play *Hockey Night in Canada* right out there on the board ice. Just a foolish outdoor game, that's all it is.

My father comes down to tell us supper is ready. He says the upper eddie is better, it has fewer rocks when the water is this low. And I tell him about the twenty-five goals I have scored this day.

My sister and I follow him home, across fields of frozen cow tracks now sprinkled with salt. We mope along on tired ankles where the winding trails of mud are black cement, then through our garden, honeycombed now. I see Oxhana climbing the hill to the Hlodan farm across the river. I see Harold Camp undressing in slanting, cluttered home that he and his mother share. In our own summer kitchen, a Christmas tree stands in a pail. Father has cut and dragged it from the swamp this very day. The old board floor of the shed cracks and snaps under our feet as we go inside to a supper we have been smelling for hours from the river.

And then, as if to take the place of board ice and hockey, or even a family meal, you appear front and centre, my sweet and tender Oxhana, just as you always do. You are still mysterious but commanding, even at this rugged age, "that time of year thou mayst in me behold." And I see you sitting there by the fire, the way you used to do in that old farmhouse, with curtains drawn against the night. Your knees are pulled up under your skirt to make a tent that covers your ankles. Your thin bare feet are resting on the edge of an empty chair, hair long over your shoulders. And your dark eyes are moving me. Even now. I share your lighted candle, hear your chamber music as you get up, and once again we move together in a kind of dance.

Rain turns to hail and filters among the trees to hop about on dead leaves and hiss in the moving river and make my bonfire smoulder. Once again you have helped me block out the hollowness, the rain, the approaching darkness. I wait for the night with an indifference that only borders on sanity. While in the trees, the little jay chirps *tweet-tweet*, its ruffled plumage delicate now upon bare limbs. It teeters in the storm, its tailfeathers the marks of a broom in swept snow.

Books by Wayne Curtis

Currents in the Stream
One Indian Summer
Fishing The Miramichi
River Guides of Miramichi
Preferred Lies
Last Stand
River Stories

Praise for Curtis' work

"A seductive storyteller wholly immersed in the world he vividly creates, Curtis reveals himself to be a lyrical and sensuous stylist."
The Globe and Mail

"Curtis' prose is more true-to-life than most current short fiction."
Quill and Quire

"Curtis' latest writings have admitted him to the company of Buckler, MacLeod, and Richards."
New Brunswick Reader